Readers' Theater, Grade 6: Science and Social Studies Topics

Contents

Introduction 2
Features 3
Index of Reading Comprehension
  and Fluency Skills 6
Correlation to Standards 7

Blackline Masters
Individual Fluency Record 8
Word Web 9
T-Chart 10
Venn Diagram 11
Main Idea Web 12

Unit 1: Science
Survivors 13
   A six-character play about four young people who are dealing with the aftermath of an earthquake.

Adaptations in Africa 32
   A six-character play about family members who compare what they learned about animals at the zoo and in Africa.

Who Calls the Shots? 51
   A six-character play about a boy who has a strange daydream due to his worries about being too short.

Unit 2: Social Studies
The Mummy's Curse 70
   A six-character play about a family visiting an Egyptian tomb and making an amazing discovery.

The Writing Is on the Wall 89
   A six-character play about a class field trip to the Museum of Archaeology.

Sojourner Truth 108
   A six-character play about students who are working on a project about Sojourner Truth, a former slave who inspired many abolitionists.

Answer Key 127

Introduction

Readers' Theater: Science and Social Studies is a program that provides engaging fluency instruction for all your readers!

Students at different reading levels
- Practice the same selections
- Pursue the same instructional goals
- Interact and build fluency together!

Students build fluency through readers' theater plays on science or social studies topics.

Each play has four to six character roles at different reading levels (measured by the Flesch-Kincaid readability scale). Use the reading levels as a guide, not a rule. In some instances, the readability levels may be somewhat misleading, as they are determined in part by syllable count. If a multi-syllable word is repeated frequently in a character's role, the role appears to be at a high reading level. Once the student masters the word, that part of the role is no longer as challenging.

The instructional power of the small mixed-ability group is at the heart of this program. Each play and lesson plan has been carefully designed to promote meaningful group interaction. In contrast to independent reading, readers using *Readers' Theater* build skills in a rich environment of peer-to-peer modeling, discussion, and feedback.

The program provides a clear, structured approach to building fluency, vocabulary, and comprehension. The key to developing skills is practice. Each lesson provides that practice through a routine of five instructionally focused rehearsals.

1. The first rehearsal focuses on familiarizing the students with the overall text.
2. The Vocabulary Rehearsal involves students in various activities focusing on vocabulary words. Use the Word Web blackline on page 9 to help students master the vocabulary.
3. The Fluency Rehearsal provides explicit fluency instruction focused on one of the following skill areas:
   - Phrasing Properly
   - Reading with Word Accuracy
   - Using Expression
   - Using Punctuation
4. The Comprehension Rehearsal provides explicit comprehension instruction focused on one of the following skill areas:
   - Asking Questions
   - Building Background
   - Identifying Main Idea
   - Making Connections
   - Making Inferences
   - Monitoring Comprehension
   - Summarizing
   - Visualizing
5. The Final Rehearsal brings it all together.

Following the Final Rehearsal, students will be able to perform the play with great confidence and success. Use the Individual Fluency Record on page 8 to provide students with positive feedback.

Features

Summary of play

Readability level for each role

Listing of the lesson's instructional focuses and key vocabulary

Teacher Read Aloud: Use the Read Aloud to introduce the play's topics or themes while modeling good fluency.

Instructional Warm-Ups: Provide focused pre-reading instruction that includes strategies for fluency and comprehension.

Sojourner Truth

Summary

"Sojourner Truth" is a six-character play about students who are working on a project about Sojourner Truth, a former slave who inspired many abolitionists.

Meet the Players

Character	Reading Level
Narrator	3.7
Kendi	3.2
Berto	4.4
Ines	4.7
Hidori	2.3
Sojourner Truth	3.6

Fluency Focus
Reading with Word Accuracy

Comprehension Focus
Summarizing

Vocabulary
antislavery
auction
autobiography
convention
involved
passion
sue

Read Aloud Tip

Introduce the fluency focus of **reading with word accuracy**. Write *reformers* and *abolitionists* on the board. Point out that good readers think about how to pronounce difficult words before they read aloud. They look at each word part and then put the parts together. Have students read each word with you, first stressing the separate syllables and then reading each whole word aloud.

Set the Stage

Teacher Read Aloud *pages 110–111*
This selection is about social reform in the United States and some of the individuals who fought injustice. Ask students to listen carefully as you read the selection aloud.

Get Ready

Vocabulary *page 112*
Use this page to introduce important vocabulary. Discuss the Word Play feature, focusing on helping students connect the words to their own background and experience.

Fluency and Comprehension Warm-Ups *pages 113–114*
Review these pages with students. Use the following for students who need additional help with the concepts:

- **Reading with Word Accuracy** When you come to unfamiliar words, remember to look for parts of the word that you know. Put the parts together to say a word that makes sense. Then practice saying the word. Try doing this with words from the Read Aloud, such as *petitions* and *salvation*.
- **Summarizing** Summarizing is retelling the important parts of what you read. Look at paragraph 4 of the Read Aloud. Name two or three of the most important ideas in the paragraph. Put those ideas together in a one-sentence summary of the paragraph.

www.harcourtschoolsupply.com
© Harcourt Achieve Inc. All rights reserved.
108
Sojourner Truth
Readers' Theater 6, SV 9781419031717

Relevant Student Pages

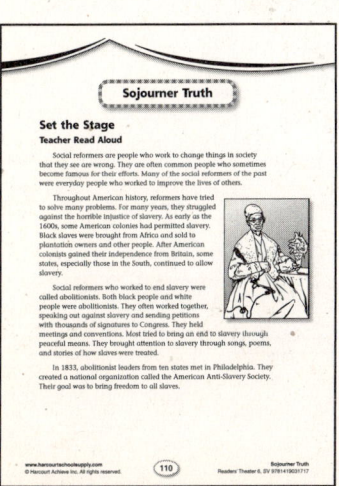

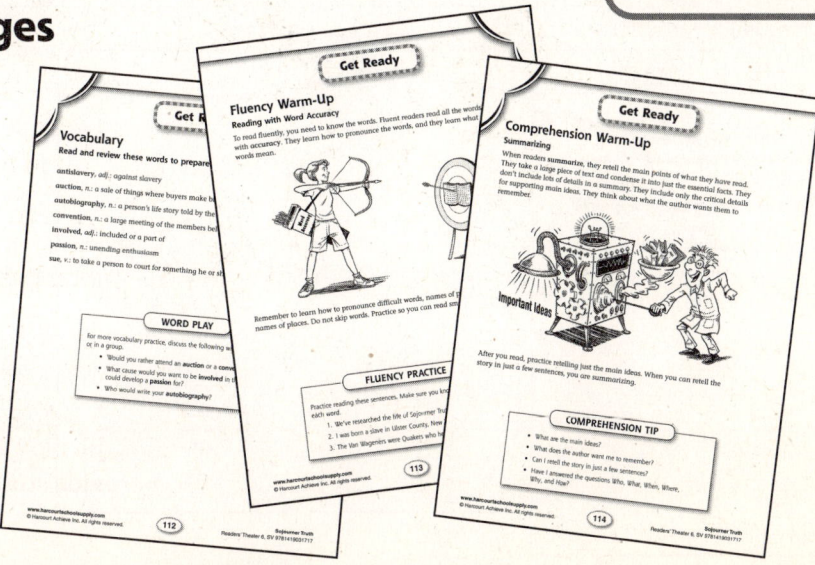

Features, continued

Opportunity for students to build confidence before beginning group work

Tip for engaging student groups in another meaningful vocabulary activity

Routine of five rehearsals, the heart of the lesson. The routine breaks the complex process of oral reading down into simple, manageable activities, each with its own instructional focus.

Sojourner Truth pages 115–124

Independent Practice
Set up the groups and assign each student a part. Then have students read through their assigned parts once before small group practice begins.

Small Group Practice
Assemble the groups. You may want to use the following rehearsal schedule. Each rehearsal, which should involve a complete oral read-through, has an activity to guide students.

1. **First Rehearsal:** Invite students to scan the entire play to find italicized stage directions. Remind students that these directions tell actors how to speak or what to do. Discuss the reason for having the narrator and Sojourner sit separately from the other actors. Then ask students to read together as a group for the first time.

2. **Vocabulary Rehearsal:** Have students locate the vocabulary words used in the play and write each word on a separate index card. Then have students take turns choosing a card, reading the word aloud, and using the word in a sentence.

3. **Fluency Rehearsal:** Reading with Word Accuracy Before this rehearsal, review the fluency instruction on page 113. Remind students to pay attention to the Fluency Tips as they read. Then, after the rehearsal, ask each student to choose one tip and apply it to an example from the play. For example, the tip on page 117 could be used with the names *Ulster* and *Isabella* on that page.

4. **Comprehension Rehearsal:** Summarizing After this rehearsal, have students work together in groups to complete a Story Map that identifies important events in Sojourner Truth's life. Remind students that the Story Map should include just facts. It should not include details. Then challenge groups to use the Story Map as a guide for writing a four- or five-sentence biographical sketch of Sojourner.

5. **Final Rehearsal:** Observe this rehearsal, focusing on students' ability to read with word accuracy. For example, do actors look for word parts they recognize to accurately read names, such as *Van Wagener* and *Dumont*?

Performance
This is your opportunity to sit back, relax, and enjoy the performance. Encourage students to have fun while performing!

Curtain Call pages 125–126
Assign these questions and activities for students to complete either independently or in a group.

Vocabulary Tip
For more vocabulary practice, have students discuss the following:
- If you sit on the sidelines at a sports event, how can you still be **involved** in the game?
- What are some reasons people **sue** individuals or companies?
- Name another word that includes the prefix *anti-*, as in **antislavery**. What does the word mean?

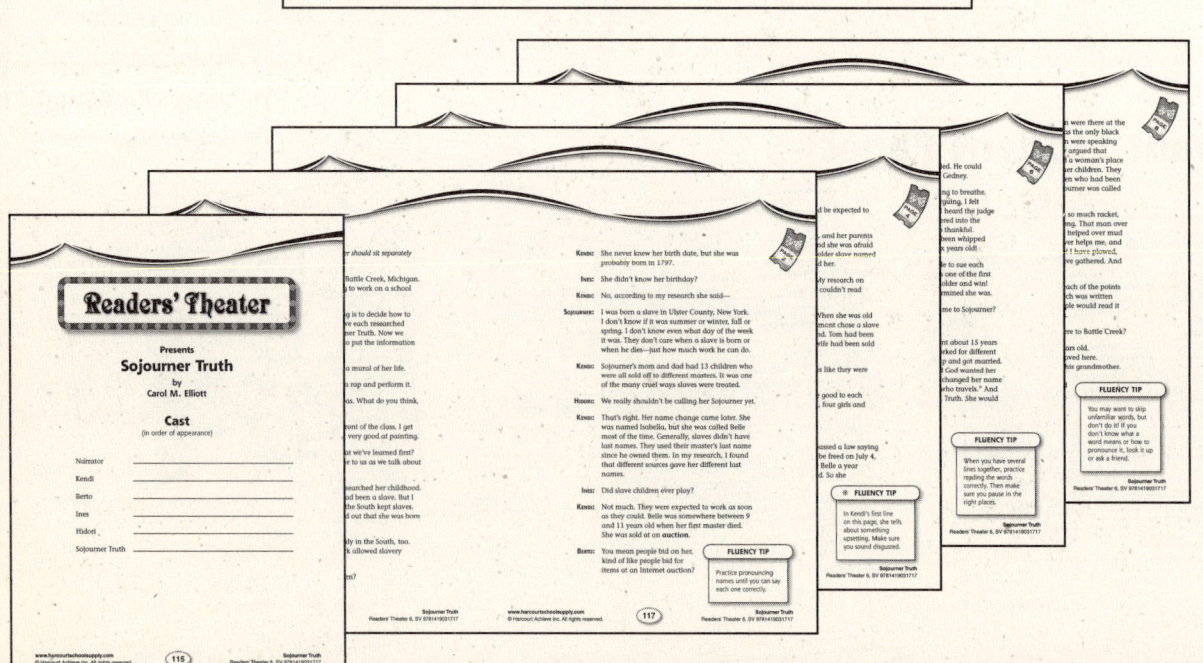

Features, continued

Comprehension questions ranging from literal to inferential →

Comprehension

Write your answer to each question on the lines below.

1. What were two ways Belle's masters were cruel to her?

2. How did Sojourner help the antislavery movement?

3. Why do you think Sojourner went to see President Lincoln?

4. How do you think the men at the women's rights convention felt when Sojourner got up to speak?

5. Do you think Sojourner chose the right name when she changed her name?

6. What do you admire most about Sojourner Truth?

7. What are two ways in which your life would be different if you couldn't read and write?

8. Why do you think Sojourner was able to influence people to join the fight against slavery?

Vocabulary

Write the vocabulary word that answers each question.

| passion | convention | auction | sue |
| involved | antislavery | autobiography | |

1. Which word names a way to sell something?
2. In what movement would an abolitionist participate?
3. What would you call an account you write about your own life?
4. Which word describes an intense feeling?
5. Which word describes a large meeting?

← **Vocabulary items testing students' understanding, not their ability to identify verbatim definitions**

Extension

1. With a partner, choose a social reformer to research. Then present your findings to the class.
   - Find out what the reformer did and summarize it for the class.
   - Why was he or she successful at what he or she did?
   - How can you connect what he or she did to your life?

2. Discuss this question in a small group: "How would social reformers work to improve the lives of people today?"
   - Think about problems you know of in the world.
   - What could people do to help?
   - What could you do to help?

← **Extension activities for additional interaction, involvement, research, writing, and creativity. Use the blackline masters provided on pages 9–12 to help students complete these extension activities.**

Index of Reading Comprehension and Fluency Skills

Reading Comprehension Skills

Skill	Play	Pages
Asking Questions	The Mummy's Curse	70–88
Building Background	Who Calls the Shots?	51–69
Identifying Main Idea	The Writing Is on the Wall	89–107
Making Inferences	Adaptations in Africa	32–50
Summarizing	Sojourner Truth	108–126
Visualizing	Survivors	13–31

Fluency Skills

Skill	Play	Pages
Proper Phrasing	The Mummy's Curse	70–88
Reading with Word Accuracy	Who Calls the Shots?	51–69
	Sojourner Truth	108–126
Using Expression	Adaptations in Africa	32–50
	The Writing Is on the Wall	89–107
Using Punctuation	Survivors	13–31

Correlation to Standards

Unit 1: Science

Survivors *Pages 13–31*

Health Standard: Knows injury-prevention and injury-management strategies for personal and family health

Adaptations in Africa *Pages 32–50*

Science Standard: Identifies adaptations of plants and animals that allow them to live in specific environments

Who Calls the Shots? *Pages 51–69*

Science Standard: Describes how the various systems of living organisms work together to perform a vital function

Unit 2: Social Studies

The Mummy's Curse *Pages 70–88*

Social Studies Standard: Describes the characteristics of ancient civilizations, with emphasis on the cultural and scientific contributions, including writing systems, calendars, and building of monuments

The Writing Is on the Wall *Pages 89–107*

Social Studies Standard: Describes the characteristics of ancient civilizations, with emphasis on the cultural and scientific contributions, including writing systems, calendars, and building of monuments

Sojourner Truth *Pages 108–126*

Social Studies Standard: Knows significant aspects of the lives and accomplishments of selected men and women in the historical period of ancient civilizations to the present day

Name: _____   Date: _____

Individual Fluency Record

	Needs Improvement	Satisfactory	Excellent
Expression			
Uses correct intonation for statements			
Uses correct intonation for questions			
Uses correct intonation for commands			
Uses correct intonation for exclamations			
Interjects character's emotions and moods			
Reads words in all capitals to express character's emotions			
Reads words in dark print to express character's emotions			
Reads onomatopoeia words to mimic character			
Volume			
Uses appropriate loudness			
Voice reflects tone of character			
Voice reflects feelings of character			
Accuracy			
Reads words accurately			
Speed			
Reads sentences smoothly with line breaks			
Reads words in short sentences as meaningful units			
Reads phrases and clauses as meaningful units			
Reads rhyming text at a constant speed			
Reads rhythmic text with a constant beat			
Punctuation			
Pauses at the end of sentences			
Pauses at commas that follow introductory phrases			
Pauses at commas in series			
Pauses at commas in clauses			
Pauses at commas after introductory names			
Pauses at ellipses			
Pauses at dashes			
Recognizes that question marks are questions			
Recognizes that exclamation points indicate strong feeling			
General			
Demonstrates confidence			
Feels at ease in front of an audience			
Speaks without being prompted			
Speaks at the appropriate time for the character's part			
Demonstrates the character's personality			

Teacher Comments

Name _____ Date _____

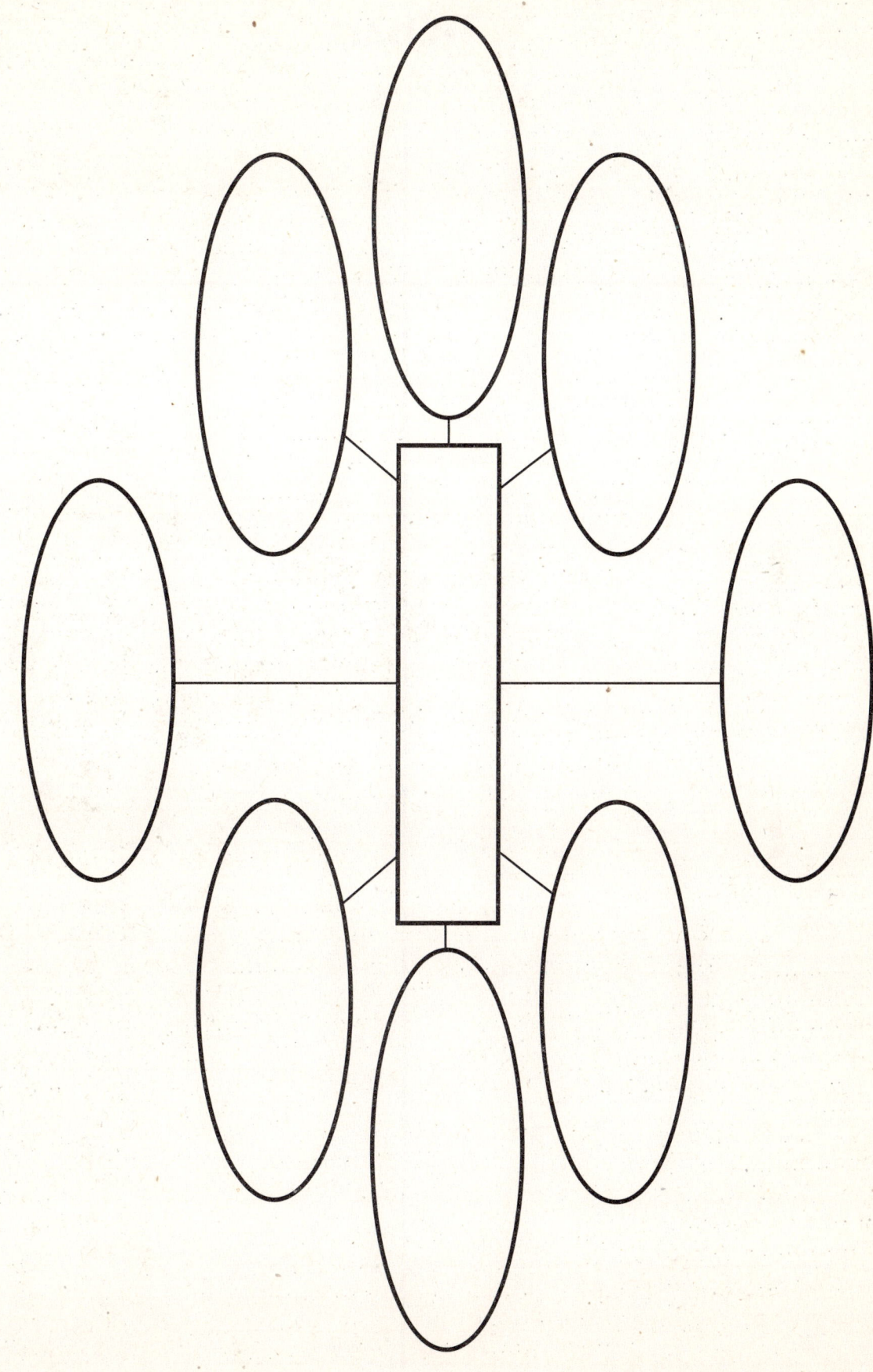

Word Web

www.harcourtschoolsupply.com
© Harcourt Achieve Inc. All rights reserved.

Blackline Master: Word Web
Readers' Theater 6, SV 9781419031717

Name   Date

T-Chart

Name _____ Date _____

Venn Diagram

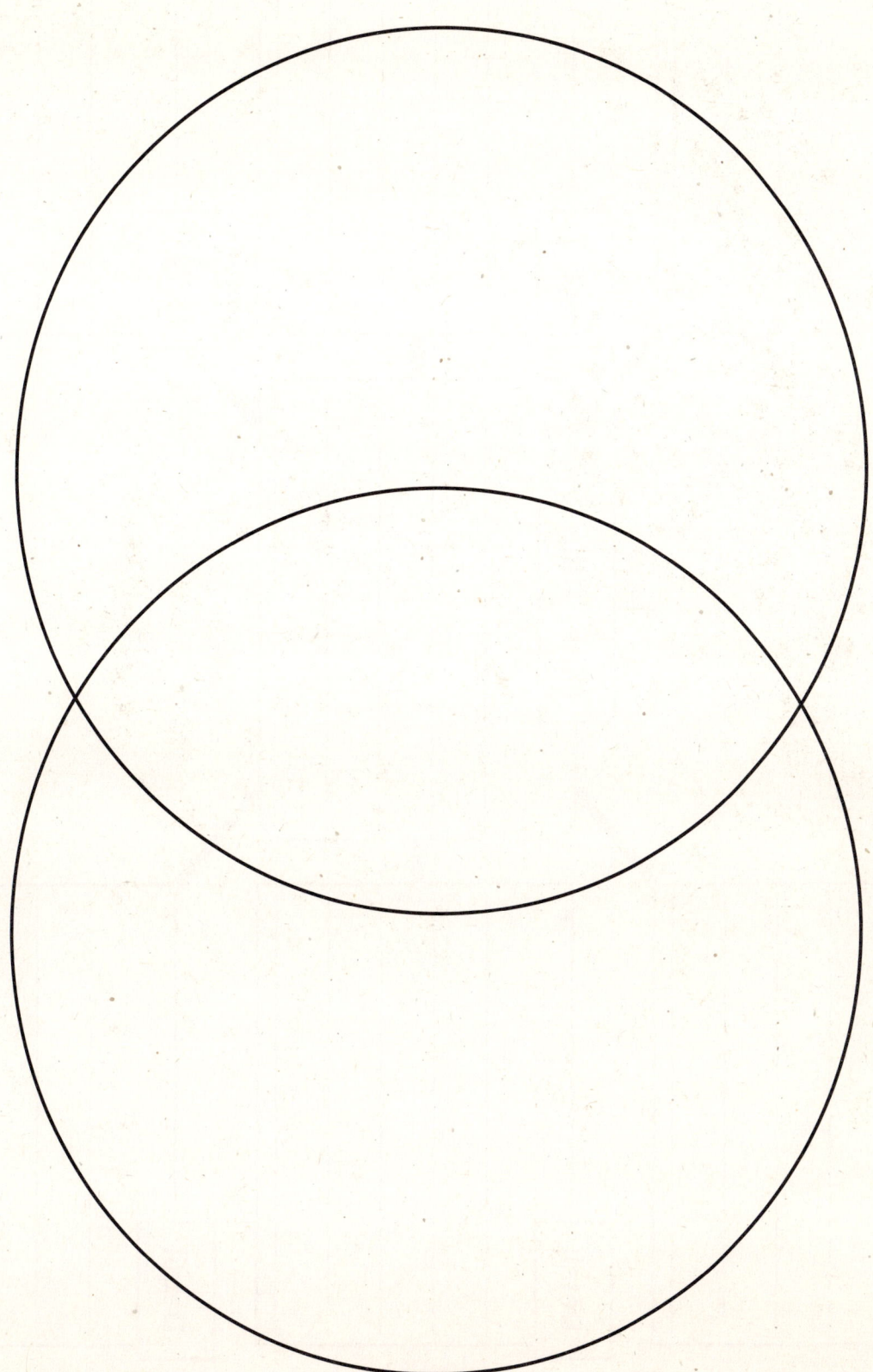

Name _____ Date _____

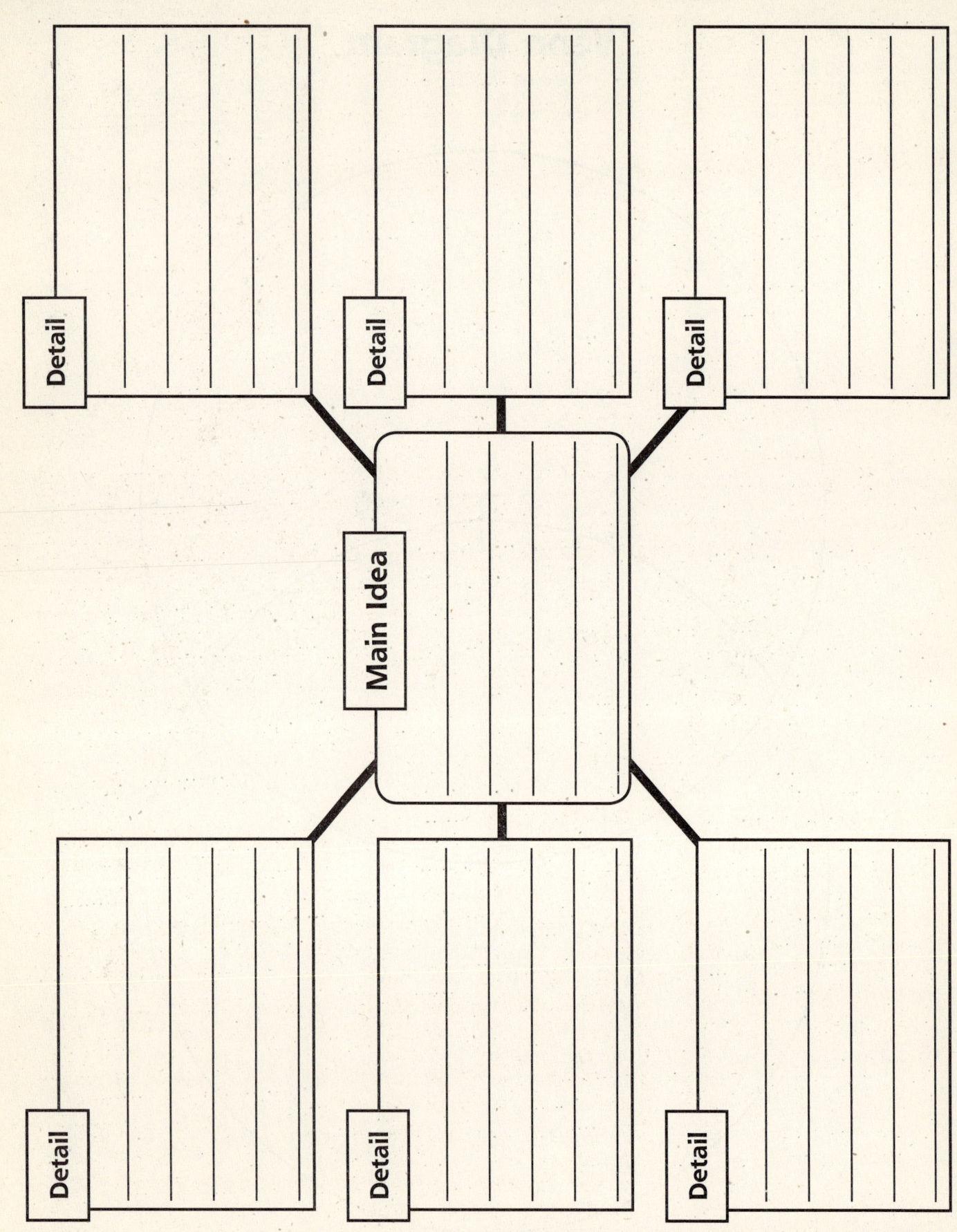

Survivors

Summary
"Survivors" is a six-character play about four young people who are dealing with the aftermath of an earthquake.

Meet the Players

Character	Reading Level
Julia	4.5
Timothy	1.0
Narrator 1	3.5
Narrator 2	6.0
Joey	2.3
Sophia	0.8

Fluency Focus
Using Punctuation

Comprehension Focus
Visualizing

Vocabulary
aftershock
durable
essentials
flustered
foresight
fragments
hunkered

Read Aloud Tip
Read the selection aloud. Next introduce the fluency focus of **using punctuation**. Then reread paragraph 3 of the Read Aloud, focusing on stopping at each period. Read the paragraph again. This time, ask students to listen and note how many sentences they hear by keeping a tally of the sentences on a sheet of scratch paper.

Set the Stage

Teacher Read Aloud pages 15–16
This selection is about the science of fires and what to do if you are in a building that catches fire. Ask students to listen for pauses indicated by commas and dashes as you read the selection aloud.

Get Ready

Vocabulary page 17
Use this page to introduce important vocabulary. Discuss the Word Play feature, focusing on helping students connect the words to their own background and experiences.

Fluency and Comprehension Warm-Ups pages 18–19
Review these pages with students. Use the following for students who need additional help with the concepts:

- **Using Punctuation** Paying attention to punctuation helps you know how to read a selection. When you come to a dash, pause slightly longer than when you come to a comma. Study the Read Aloud to find sentences with both a dash and a comma. Choose one sentence to read aloud, pausing at each dash and comma.

- **Visualizing** Visualizing is creating pictures in your mind as you read. It means thinking about what your senses might tell you if you were part of a scene. For example, when the Read Aloud describes escaping from a burning house, think about the heat, the crackling of the fire, and the scent of smoke. Draw a picture of what you are visualizing in your mind.

Survivors *pages 20–29*

Independent Practice
Set up the groups and assign each student a part. Then have students read through their assigned parts once before small group practice begins.

Small Group Practice
Assemble the groups. You may want to use the following rehearsal schedule. Each rehearsal, which should involve a complete oral read-through, has an activity to guide students.

Vocabulary Tip

For more vocabulary practice, have students discuss the following:

- What are two things you consider **essential** at school? At home?
- If someone **hunkered** down near you, would you expect him or her to stay for a while?
- How is a **fragment** similar to a fraction?

1. First Rehearsal: Invite students to read the title and cast of characters and to scan the play. Ask volunteers to predict what happens to the characters. Then have students read together as a group for the first time.

2. Vocabulary Rehearsal: Have students locate and list all of the vocabulary words used in the play. Provide them with copies of the Word Web on page 9. Ask them to work in their groups to create a Word Web using one vocabulary word. Remind them that a Word Web can include definitions, examples, things related to the word, and so on. Provide time for groups to share their Word Webs.

3. Fluency Rehearsal: **Using Punctuation** During this rehearsal, encourage students to pay attention to the Fluency Tips. After the rehearsal, invite each student to choose one line with an exclamation point or an ellipsis to read aloud to the group.

4. Comprehension Rehearsal: **Visualizing** Guide students to focus on creating pictures in their minds as they read. After the reading, ask them to draw one scene or event they visualized. Have students share their drawings.

5. Final Rehearsal: Observe this rehearsal, focusing on students' awareness of punctuation. For example, when Julia speaks her first lines on page 21, does the student actor's voice rise at the end of each question?

Performance
This is your opportunity to sit back, relax, and enjoy the performance. Encourage students to have fun while performing!

Curtain Call *pages 30–31*
Assign these questions and activities for students to complete either independently or in a group.

Survivors

Set the Stage

Teacher Read Aloud

"FIRE!"

Before you do anything, let's examine just what fire is and what to do if a fire breaks out in your home.

Fire is a natural phenomenon that happens when a combustible fuel comes into contact with oxygen and exceptionally high temperatures. Fire is a chemical reaction that turns fuel to gas, and flames are the visual indication of the gas being heated.

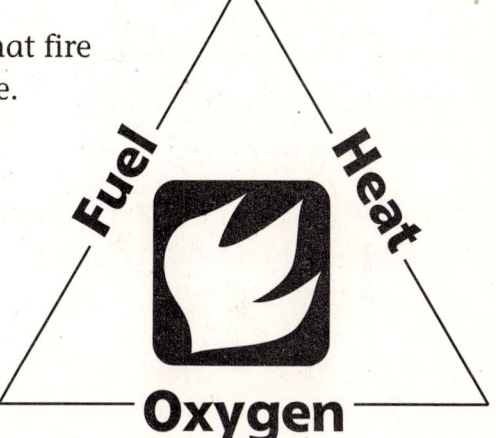

Think of fire in terms of a regular triangle—three equal sides made up of fuel, heat, and oxygen. Each component, or side of the triangle, must exist in order for fire to exist. If you eliminate any one of the components of the triangle, the fire is extinguished.

We can define fuel as any type of combustible material—in other words, anything that could combust, or catch on fire. How much the object will burn depends on how much moisture it contains, its size and shape, its quantity, and its location. The amount of moisture contained in the fuel determines how easily the fuel will burn.

Heat takes the moisture out of whatever fuel is being burned. In a wildfire, for example, the fuel might be the dried brush and grasses. Additionally, the heat warms up the surrounding air and preheats any fuel immediately adjacent to the burn site, allowing the fire to spread.

The last component of the triangle is oxygen. Most fires need at least 16 percent oxygen to burn. Air contains about 21 percent oxygen. That means that fires need air to continue burning. When the fuel burns and reacts with the oxygen around it, it releases more heat.

So what do you do if you're caught in a building on fire?

First, get out fast. Every second counts! In under a minute, a house can fill with thick, black smoke and become engulfed in flames. If your family has done its homework, you've practiced an escape plan from every room in your house. And that practice includes doing it with your eyes closed, too!

Forget Aunt Heloise's swan-shaped lamp. Forget your favorite stuffed animal. Forget what you think might be essential items to have. Don't waste time gathering possessions. Most can be replaced.

Before you open a closed door, feel around it with the back of your hand (it's much more sensitive than the palm side). Feel the top of the door, the doorknob, and the space between the door and the door frame. If it feels hot, don't open it—use your secondary escape plan. If you do open it and smoke or heat comes in, shut it again.

And last but not least, once you are out, STAY OUT! Call 911 for help.

In this play, you will read about how to survive a disaster. Along the way, you will practice your reading. Use the vocabulary and warm-ups on the next three pages to help you get ready to read.

Get Ready

Vocabulary

Read and review these words to prepare for reading the play.

aftershock, *n.*: one of several lesser shocks that follow the main shock of an earthquake

durable, *adj.*: able to withstand wear and decay

essentials, *n.*: those things that are absolutely necessary to have

flustered, *v.* or *adj.*: (made) nervous, excited, or confused

foresight, *n.*: the ability to see and prepare for what is likely to happen in the future

fragments, *n.*: pieces of something

hunkered, *v.*: settled in for a period of time

WORD PLAY

For more vocabulary practice, discuss the following with a partner or in a group.

- When have you felt **flustered**? Why did you feel that way?
- Discuss a time when you had the **foresight** to make an alternate plan.
- Why might you need **durable** gear for a camping trip?

Get Ready

Fluency Warm-Up
Using Punctuation

As a fluent reader, you should **use punctuation** to help you understand and remember what you read. Pause at commas. Change your voice when you see a question mark or an exclamation point. If a sentence is a long one, paying attention to the punctuation will help to break up the sentence into smaller, more understandable parts.

Practice reading aloud to a friend or family member, using the punctuation as a guide. If what you're reading is smooth, clear, and understandable to your audience, then you are probably using the punctuation correctly.

FLUENCY PRACTICE

Read aloud the following unpunctuated paragraph. Then write the paragraph, adding the correct punctuation. Read the punctuated paragraph, making sure to note the difference punctuation makes in your reading.

Fire screamed the man in the burning building what are we to do the only way out is to jump but I'm too afraid to do that so now I don't know what to do look there's a door that's open it's not hot I think we can get out are you coming with us

_____

_____

_____

_____

Get Ready

Comprehension Warm-Up

Visualizing

Visualizing means using the words you read or hear to paint pictures in your mind. These pictures help you imagine what a character, a place, or a thing looks like. Visualizing will help you understand and remember what you read.

So when you read, listen for words that describe what someone or something looks like. Listen for action words that tell what's happening. Compare what you're reading or hearing to something you already know. The result will be a picture in your mind. And you can change the picture as you read!

COMPREHENSION TIP

Visualize what you are reading by asking yourself the following questions.

- What does the character, place, or thing look like?
- How does it sound?
- What is it doing?
- What does it remind me of?

Readers' Theater

Presents
Survivors
by
Judy Kentor Schmauss

Cast
(in order of appearance)

Julia   _____

Timothy   _____

Narrator 1   _____

Narrator 2   _____

Joey   _____

Sophia   _____

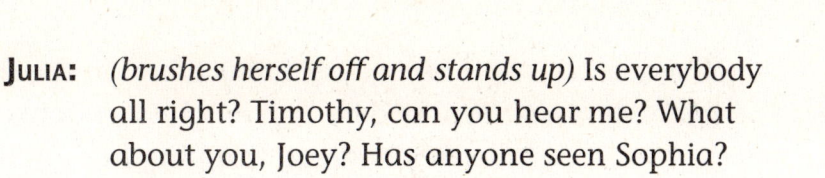

JULIA: *(brushes herself off and stands up)* Is everybody all right? Timothy, can you hear me? What about you, Joey? Has anyone seen Sophia?

TIMOTHY: *(moves a lamp off his lap and uprights a small table that had fallen down)* I'm here. I'm OK. I'm just a little banged up. What happened? Was that an earthquake?

NARRATOR 1: It had started out as a normal day. The four teens had gone to a movie and had returned to Julia and Joey's house. Their parents were at a friend's house for the evening.

NARRATOR 2: It was getting late. Timothy and Sophia were getting ready to leave, when a violent earthquake suddenly shook the residence.

JOEY: *(stands up and uses his foot to move debris out of his way)* I guess I'm all right, too, but I don't know where Sophia is. I remember seeing her head toward the guest bathroom when the quake started.

JULIA: We've got to locate her! Sophia! Can you hear me?

TIMOTHY: I think I heard a noise. It was coming from near the dining room. Come on! Help me look! *(Walks over fallen objects and into the dining room.)*

JOEY: Sophia, are you all right or are you hurt? Can you hear me? *(Joey is standing in the dining room, looking at Sophia, who is lying on the floor.)* Hey, everyone, I found her over by the dining room, under the bookcase. Hang on a minute, Sophia, and we'll get you out of there!

Narrator 2: A frightened Sophia is lying on the floor, surrounded by broken glass. A bookcase has fallen on her legs, trapping her underneath. Books are scattered everywhere.

Sophia: My legs hurt where the bookcase fell on me. I think I'm OK.

Joey: Don't try to move, Sophia. Timothy, how about getting over to the other side so we can try to lift the bookcase off her? Julia, you move up here to the top end of the bookcase.

Timothy: We've got to move these books and broken glass first. *(Julia, Timothy, and Joey move as much as they can.)* You say when, Joey.

Julia: I really apologize, Sophia. I told my parents that the bookcase should be bolted to the wall, like Mrs. Simpson said at school. I suppose they totally forgot about doing it. I don't think they bolted down anything!

Joey: On my count . . . 1, 2, 3 . . . lift!

Narrator 1: The boys struggle with the heavy bookcase. At first it won't budge, but they don't accept defeat.

Timothy: We're getting it! Can you get out of there?

Sophia: I'm trying, but my legs hurt. And don't be silly, Julia. An earthquake is no one's fault.

FLUENCY TIP

There are a lot of exclamation points in these first pages. Make sure you read the sentences that end this way with excitement and enthusiasm or with the appropriate emotion.

JOEY: Julia, we've got the bookcase, so grab Sophia under her arms and drag her out. But watch out for the broken glass.

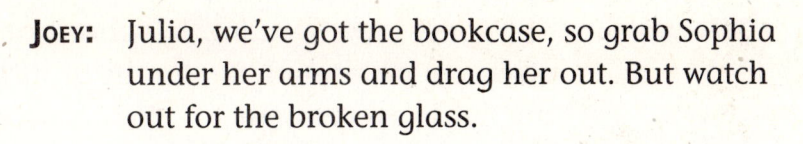

NARRATOR 2: The boys' arms shake with the effort of supporting the bookcase. Julia manages to pull Sophia to safety. As she clears Sophia's feet from the last inch of the fallen bookcase, the boys release their grip. *(The bookcase crashes to the floor.)*

JULIA: Let's carefully pick her up and carry her to the living room sofa. Then I can examine her legs for fractures or broken bones. Timothy, look underneath the kitchen sink for the first-aid kit. It has all the **essentials**.

TIMOTHY: Sure thing! I'm really glad you took that first-aid class last year.

✻ **JULIA:** If we cover her and keep her still and quiet, we should be able to keep her from going into shock. Somebody grab some comforters off the beds. But PLEASE make sure you're careful when you go into the bedrooms!

JOEY: Rats, the telephone is out! My cell phone isn't connecting either. There's clearly no way to get in touch with Mom and Dad or anybody else. I'll be back in a few minutes. I'm going to check the situation outside.

NARRATOR 1: Joey tries to open the front door, but it falls away from him, crashing onto the front porch. The crash makes dust spit up everywhere. The tree that used to be in their front yard is now on the porch.

> ✻ **FLUENCY TIP**
>
> The word PLEASE is written in all caps. That means the word should be emphasized when you read it.

Narrator 2: The street is eerily quiet. Telephone and electrical poles are lying on the ground. Sparks are flying everywhere.

Joey: This is completely crazy! Where is everybody? There must be families who are trapped in their houses.

Timothy: He's right. Here's the kit. I'll be right back with the blankets. How are Sophia's legs? *(Timothy goes into one of the bedrooms. He returns with two blankets.)*

Julia: I think one of them is broken, so she can't be moved for a while. We'll need something to splint her leg to keep it from moving until we can get her to the hospital. If we can get to the freezer, we can put ice on her other leg to keep the swelling down.

Timothy: What can we use as a splint? Gosh, I wish Mom and Dad were here. They'd know what to do!

Julia: What about one of the shelves from the bookcase that fell? They're pretty **durable**. Why don't you investigate and see if one is usable?

Joey: Be patient one more minute, Julia, while I move some of this garbage around so I can check it out. *(Joey finds only one whole shelf.)* Here's one. It's the only one that didn't break. I hope it'll work.

Julia: Fantastic, Joey. Thanks! I think it will be exactly what I need. If you could get me one more thing, I'd really appreciate it—a sheet from one of the smaller beds. I'll rip it up into long rectangular strips that we can use to tie the splint onto Sophia's broken leg.

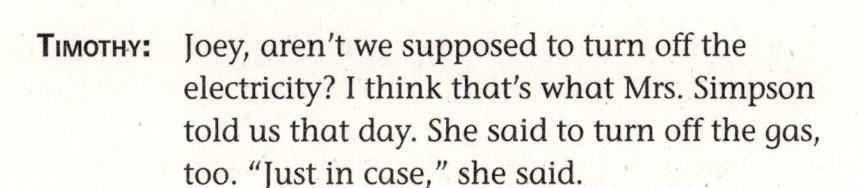

Timothy: Joey, aren't we supposed to turn off the electricity? I think that's what Mrs. Simpson told us that day. She said to turn off the gas, too. "Just in case," she said.

Joey: Right! I almost forgot one of the most important things she said! We have to turn everything off, just in case something falls over and starts a fire. I'll look around and make sure nothing's on fire. The last thing we need to have is a fire. I think I remember the way that Dad showed me to turn everything off. I'll be back upstairs in a few minutes. *(Joey leaves to check out the basement and turn everything off.)*

Sophia: PLEASE be careful, Joey! Yell if you need help.

Timothy: I'll try to find some flashlights. I'll look for more blankets we can use, too. Do you know where your folks keep extra batteries? What about a radio?

Julia: I put all the essentials together in a box under my bed. I packed it right after Mrs. Simpson gave us that lecture about what should go in an earthquake survival kit. Gosh, I never thought I'd actually have to use it!

Narrator 1: Just that week, the kids had gotten a lecture from their teacher. It was on earthquake survival. They lived in an area prone to earthquakes. Julia had taken it to heart.

Narrator 2: Julia takes most things quite seriously. Last year her teacher suggested that one person in every family should know first aid. She signed up right away for a first-aid class. Her **foresight** has paid off in this survival situation.

Joey: *(yelling from the basement)* Someone throw down the fire extinguisher from up there! Hurry up!

Timothy: Here I come! *(Timothy goes down the stairs holding the fire extinguisher. He and Joey put out a small fire. Then they come back up the stairs.)*

Joey: That was close. It was just a small fire that started because the water heater fell over. I'm glad we remembered that we should do that—shut everything off, that is. Otherwise, we might not have discovered the fire until it was too late. I'm going to remind Dad to bolt the water heater to the wall!

Sophia: I'm so thirsty. Is there any water around? I am feeling kind of weak.

Timothy: What about bottled water? Did you guys get any? Mrs. Simpson said we should have three gallons per person! That's what I told my parents. We stocked up on canned foods and bottled water. We got bandages and snacks, too.

✶ **Julia:** Hang in there, Sophia! Timothy, there should be bottled water in the pantry, but be careful when you open the door. All the canned goods might have crashed onto the floor. Sophia, you're not allergic to nuts, are you?

Sophia: No, I can eat nuts. In fact, nuts are my favorite snack.

Julia: Timothy, see if you can find some nuts, too. That will help her replenish her energy. Mom usually keeps some right on the kitchen counter.

> ✶ **FLUENCY TIP**
>
> In Julia's lines, there is a long sentence with two commas. Pause at each comma so the sentence sounds natural.

Timothy: I found lots of stuff. There's plenty for us to eat. Here, Sophia. *(Hands her the nuts.)*

Sophia: Thanks, big brother. Mom and Dad would be really proud of you.

Timothy: Thanks, Sis! Guys, if you think you should go out to rescue people, that's cool. But I think one of us should stay here with Sophia. I don't like the idea of leaving her alone here—just in case there's an **aftershock**.

Sophia: Timothy's right. Please don't leave me alone here.

Julia: We'd never leave you alone, Sophia! Let's get rid of these glass **fragments** and make sure that if there's an aftershock, nothing big will fall.

Narrator 1: The three teens try to clean up as best they can.

Joey: Julia, I think you and I should go and see if we can help anyone. You're the best one to go since you've taken first aid. Timothy, how about if you stay here with Sophia?

Timothy: I can do that.

Narrator 2: Julia and Joey walk carefully outside and onto the street. People are milling around now. Most of them look dazed, but not too badly hurt. They hear sirens in the background and know that fire engines and ambulances are on their way. Suddenly, the ground starts moving again.

Joey: Get down, Julia! Cover your face! It's an aftershock.

Julia: You, too! Gosh, I hope Sophia and Timothy will be able to manage by themselves.

Narrator 1: The ground rumbles and shakes for a few more terrifying minutes. Then everything is still. Julia and Joey hear crashing noises here and there. Dogs start barking. They hear more sirens in the distance.

Joey: Whew! I'm glad that's over! Are you OK, Jules?

❋ **Julia:** I'm fine—just a bit **flustered**. I knew there was a possibility of getting one or two of those, but it's terrifying even so. I remember Mrs. Simpson saying there could be a number of aftershocks from an earthquake like the one we had. I hope that was the last of them, although I won't be surprised if we get another one.

Joey: Neither will I. Julia, do you think Mom and Dad are all right? I think maybe we should hike over to the Palmettis'.

Julia: I'm worried about Mom and Dad, too. Let's go back inside and check on Sophia and Timothy first. Then we'll see if Mom and Dad are safe.

Narrator 2: Julia and Joey go back inside the house, where they find both Sophia and Timothy safe and sound. Sophia is still on the sofa. Timothy is **hunkered** down on the floor next to it, holding Sophia's hand.

Sophia: Are you guys OK? Did you feel that? I hate this. I hate not knowing about our families. I want to get out of here. *(Sophia begins to cry but pulls herself together.)*

> ❋ **FLUENCY TIP**
>
> Did you notice the dash in Julia's line? A dash creates emphasis. When you read a line with a dash, stop briefly at the dash. Then read what follows, using the right emotion.

TIMOTHY: I hate this, too, Soph. How about if a few of us try to get over to the Palmettis'?

JOEY: Well, Julia and I had pretty much decided that we should try to find them anyway. Let's get going.

NARRATOR 2: As Julia and Joey are preparing to help Sophia off the sofa and leave the house, they all hear urgent shouting from outside. Timothy is the first one to the door.

TIMOTHY: It's our parents! Yippee! Boy, are we ever glad to see you!

NARRATOR 1: All four parents rush to see that their children are OK. Their concern about Sophia and their relief that the others are unharmed outweigh their alarm about the damage to their houses. All that really matters is that the teenagers are safe.

NARRATOR 2: After everyone finishes hugging, Sophia's parents and brother take Sophia to the hospital. Julia and Joey's parents sit with them on the sofa. They tell them how proud they are of how the two teens and their friends handled the emergency. And then they promise to do what Mrs. Simpson had asked all the families to do. They are going to do their best to make their house as earthquake-proof as possible!

NARRATOR 1: The End!

Name _____   Date _____

Comprehension

Write your answer to each question on the lines below.

1. Why does Julia tell Timothy to be careful when he goes into the bedrooms?
   _____
   _____
   _____

2. What do the teens do to help with the immediate problems caused by the quake?
   _____
   _____
   _____

3. What do the teens do to minimize damage from an aftershock?
   _____
   _____
   _____

4. What had Julia done to prepare for an earthquake?
   _____
   _____
   _____

5. Do you agree or disagree with how the teens handle the situation? What could they do differently?
   _____
   _____
   _____

6. Where would you go for help if disaster struck and you were home alone?
   _____
   _____
   _____

7. What do you think the teens and their parents learn from their experience?
   _____
   _____
   _____

8. What is one thing you predict Julia's parents will do to make their home more earthquake-proof? _____
   _____

Name _____ Date _____

Vocabulary

Finish the story by writing a vocabulary word on each line.

> hunkered   flustered   fragments   essentials
> durable   foresight   aftershock

Gloria searched through her backpack. "I put my sunglasses in here—along with other (1) _____, like sunscreen and bottled water," she said. "I had the (2) _____ to know I'd need them on the hike."

"Oh, no!" she exclaimed, holding up two (3) _____ of plastic. "I guess cheap sunglasses aren't very (4) _____."

"Don't get (5) _____," said Tony. "I have an extra pair you can borrow."

Extension

1. Discuss the following question in a small group: "What, if any, difference would it have made if the teens' parents had been home?"
   - Would everyone have been or felt more prepared?
   - How would the teens have felt?
   - How would everyone have helped?

2. Consider the following: Suppose you had to put together an emergency survival kit. What would be included in your kit?
   - Find out what kinds of disasters are most prevalent in your area.
   - Research what kinds of objects are considered essential for a survival kit for those kinds of disasters.
   - Make a list of objects to include in your survival kit and describe briefly why they are included.

Adaptations in Africa

Summary
"Adaptations in Africa" is a six-character play about family members who compare what they learned about animals at the zoo and in Africa.

Meet the Players

Character	Reading Level
Mom	5.2
Alex	2.7
Nina	3.3
Dad	5.6
Uncle Mark	2.6
Aunt Trish	2.0

Fluency Focus
Using Expression

Comprehension Focus
Making Inferences

Vocabulary
adapt/adaptation
camouflage
gland
habitat
precaution
species

Read Aloud Tip
Read the selection once and then introduce the fluency focus, **using expression**. Ask students to close their eyes and listen to the tone and rhythm of your words as you reread several paragraphs smoothly and expressively.

Set the Stage

Teacher Read Aloud *pages 34–35*
This selection is about how animals have adapted to their surroundings. Ask students to listen carefully as you read the selection aloud.

Get Ready

Vocabulary *page 36*
Use this page to introduce important vocabulary. Discuss the Word Play feature, encouraging students to use concrete details in their responses.

Fluency and Comprehension Warm-Ups *pages 37–38*
Review these pages with students. Use the following for students who need additional help with the concepts:

- **Using Expression** Part of reading with expression is deciding what words to stress, or read with a stronger voice. Read the first sentence of the Read Aloud, stressing these important words: *many, animals, lot, water*.

- **Making Inferences** When you make inferences, you use what you read and what you already know to figure things out. What do you know about swimming and diving that helps you infer that whales have huge lungs?

Adaptations in Africa *pages 39–48*

Independent Practice
Set up the groups and assign each student a part. Then have students read through their assigned parts once before small group practice begins.

Small Group Practice
Assemble the groups. You may want to use the following rehearsal schedule. Each rehearsal, which should involve a complete oral read-through, has an activity to guide students.

1. First Rehearsal: Ask students to preview the play by reading the title, character list, and stage directions. Students should then read the play together as a group for the first time.

2. Vocabulary Rehearsal: Have students locate the vocabulary words used in the play and write each word on a separate index card. Then have students take turns choosing a card, reading the word aloud, and using the word in a sentence.

3. Fluency Rehearsal: Using Expression Before the rehearsal begins, invite students to review the Fluency Tips by alternating reading them aloud. Then encourage students to have fun by overacting—exaggerating characters' feelings.

4. Comprehension Rehearsal: Making Inferences After reading, suggest that students discuss these questions:
- From what you learned about adaptations, do you think the giraffes thousands of years ago were exactly like the giraffes today? Why or why not?
- What do you think the author wants you to learn from this play?

5. Final Rehearsal: Observe this rehearsal, focusing on students' expression. For example, when a student reads Dad's first lines on page 40, does the student sound like a parent giving a warning?

Performance
This is your opportunity to sit back, relax, and enjoy the performance. Encourage students to have fun while performing!

Curtain Call *pages 49–50*
Assign these questions and activities for students to complete either independently or in a group.

Vocabulary Tip

For more vocabulary practice, have students discuss the following:
- Name two **species** of pets.
- Describe an **adaptation** that would help human beings run faster.

Adaptations in Africa

Set the Stage
Teacher Read Aloud

Many different animals spend a lot of time under the water. These animals have special adaptations, or ways that they have adjusted to their environment.

Whales are mammals, which means they need to breathe air, just like humans. They have lungs and often must come to the water's surface to breathe. The blowhole on top of the whale's head allows the whale to breathe fresh air without coming very far out of the water. Before a whale dives under the water, it will take several deep breaths—just as you would before diving under the water. Whales have blubber to help keep them warm in very cold water. The blubber also stores food energy for the whale.

A sea otter lives most of its life in the water. Unlike the whale, the sea otter does not have blubber to keep it warm in the cold water. Air trapped in the sea otter's fur keeps it warm and helps it float. Openings in the sea otter's ears and nose close underwater. Flipper-like back feet and webbed paws help the sea otter be a great swimmer.

Penguins also spend most of their lives in the water. The only things they do on land are lay eggs and raise their chicks. Penguins have heavy, solid bones that weigh them down so they can stay under the water. Penguins also have wings that are shaped like flippers to help them swim at speeds up to 15 miles per hour. Like whales, penguins have blubber to help keep them warm. They have a gland that produces oil that they use to coat their feathers to stay waterproof.

A beaver has many adaptations to help it live in the water. Webbed feet and a flat tail help the beaver swim. A beaver's lips can close behind its front teeth, allowing it to eat underwater without getting splinters and water in its mouth. Beavers have clear eyelids and special valves in their ears and nose that close so they can see and dive under the water. Like the penguin, a beaver has an oily, waterproof coat.

A manatee resembles a walrus and is related to the elephant. Like the sea otter, a manatee does not have blubber to help keep it warm in the water. In winter, manatees seek out warmer waters. A mammal like the whale, the manatee must breathe air regularly. It can breathe air only through its nose, and its nostrils have special flaps that close tightly when it dives.

In this play, you will learn about animals and their adaptations to their environment. Use the vocabulary and warm-ups on the next three pages to help you get ready to read.

Get Ready

Vocabulary

Read and review these words to prepare for reading the play.

adapt, *v.*: to change so as to be suitable for a different condition or purpose (*n.*: **adaptation**)

camouflage, *n.*: a disguise that blends with the surroundings

gland, *n.*: an organ, tissue, or cell in the body that makes a special substance for the body to use

habitat, *n.*: the place where an animal or plant lives and grows

precaution, *n.*: a measure taken beforehand against possible danger

species, *n.*: a group of animals or plants with many common characteristics and the ability to interbreed

WORD PLAY

For more vocabulary practice, discuss the following with a partner or in a group.

- What is the natural **habitat** of a squirrel?
- What are some ways in which you have had to **adapt** to your environment?
- In what types of scenarios might a human use **camouflage**?

Get Ready

Fluency Warm-Up

Using Expression

To be a fluent reader, you need to read with **expression**. This makes reading more interesting and helps you better understand the selection. Stress certain words with your voice to read with more expression, or feeling. As you read, think about the meaning of the text. Then use the tone and rhythm of your voice to express that meaning.

Punctuation often will help you read with expression. Sometimes you'll have to think about the purpose of the sentence before you decide how to read with expression.

FLUENCY PRACTICE

Read each sentence with expression. Think about the punctuation and purpose of each sentence.

1. Where on earth did your brother run off to?
2. I am so excited that I can hardly stand it!
3. My cousin just left for a trip.
4. I think I see something lurking in the corner!

Get Ready

Comprehension Warm-Up

Making Inferences

Writers don't always tell you everything they want you to understand about a story. Sometimes you have to figure things out on your own. This is called making an **inference**. An inference is an educated guess that you make based on hints or clues in your reading.

While you are reading, think about the hints or clues that the author is giving you. This will help you understand the story and figure things out on your own.

COMPREHENSION TIP

Stop and think about hints or clues as you read. Ask yourself questions such as these.

- What information does the author give me about the characters, such as age, gender, or personality?
- What information does the author give me about the setting, such as time of day, place, or weather?
- What information does the author give me about the events in the story, such as noises, reactions, or outcomes?

Readers' Theater

Presents
Adaptations in Africa
by
Justine Dunn

Cast
(in order of appearance)

Mom _____

Alex _____

Nina _____

Dad _____

Uncle Mark _____

Aunt Trish _____

Mom: Aunt Trish just telephoned; she and Uncle Mark are driving over. They are going to bring their honeymoon album. Trish says it's crammed with photographs from their trip to San Diego.

Alex: Well, their pictures aren't going to be anywhere near as interesting as ours. I can't wait to tell them all about our trip!

Nina: I can't wait to show them the things we brought back with us. Just wait until they see my elephant necklace!

Dad: Now, kids, let's remember that Aunt Trish and Uncle Mark are just as excited to tell us about their trip as we are to tell them about ours. Please mind your manners.

Mom: Yes, you may learn something from their trip. We've never been to San Diego, but we'd like to visit someday. I've heard that San Diego has an extraordinary zoo with fascinating exhibits.

(They hear a knock on the door.)

Nina: I'll get it! *(She runs to the door.)* Hi, Aunt Trish! Hi, Uncle Mark! Come in. We were just talking about you.

Uncle Mark: All good things, I hope! How are you? I see you've grown since we saw you last.

AUNT TRISH: Hi, sweetie! It's so good to see you. Did you have fun on your trip?

ALEX: Did she have fun? She hasn't stopped talking about it since we got home! I think she started to **adapt** to Africa a little too well!

DAD: Well, hello to the newlyweds! How is married life treating you? Did you enjoy your adventure out west?

AUNT TRISH: Hey, big brother! It's good to see you. We had a wonderful trip.

UNCLE MARK: I was afraid I would have to leave Trish at the zoo. She didn't want to come home.

(The group laughs.)

MOM: What's this I hear about Trish wanting to take up residence at the zoo? Did you see some of your two-legged or four-legged family members there? *(She laughs.)* Sometimes I think about sending the kids special delivery to the zoo so they can live among their relatives.

ALEX: Very funny, Mom. Are those relatives on Dad's side or yours? *(He winks at Nina.)*

NINA: I'm guessing she's talking about the bears, which are just as hairy as Dad. Of course, some animals are always cleaning their **habitats**, just like Mom!

> **FLUENCY TIP**
>
> Notice the exclamation points in this play. An exclamation point can represent excitement, fear, or another strong emotion. Think about the purpose of the statement when reading it.

Dad: We saw plenty of our relatives in Africa, then. I couldn't believe how many different **species** of animals were living in the rain forests and deserts.

Aunt Trish: I'll bet we saw some of the same species at the zoo.

Uncle Mark: The animals live a different life in the zoo. Someone is there to feed them and take care of them all the time.

Mom: Why don't we compare animals from both trips to find out the similarities and differences? We can learn from each other's experiences.

All: Great idea!

Nina: We certainly saw a lot of giraffes, didn't we? I was used to seeing them at the zoo, but they are much more interesting in the wild.

Alex: Yeah, now I know why they are so tall. They have to reach the leaves, twigs, and fruit on the tall trees.

Dad: Over the years, giraffes with longer necks could reach food others couldn't reach. They were more likely to survive and pass on their traits to their offspring. That is called an **adaptation**. The giraffe also can go without drinking water for several weeks. We saw many animals that have adjusted to their environments in order to survive.

Aunt Trish: We saw giraffes at the zoo, but I doubt they have to go without water.

Uncle Mark: There are trees that the giraffes can eat from, but zookeepers also feed them.

Mom: Giraffes also use their long upper lip and their tongue to gather their food. Their outstretched tongue is about 21 inches long!

Alex: Yuck—I would hate to be licked by a giraffe! Its tongue is rough and purple or black in color. It's kind of gross.

Nina: Oh, but they are so cute! I love the color of their coat! The pattern helps protect them by making them hard to see when they stand among the trees.

Uncle Mark: The giraffes you saw were wearing coats? We didn't see that at the zoo. *(Laughs at his own joke.)*

Aunt Trish: Oh, Mark, don't be such a goof.

Dad: Yet another adaptation for the giraffe is called **camouflage**. Many animals have coloring that helps them hide from their enemies.

Mom: Because the giraffe lives in the desert, it can close its nostrils completely to keep out dust and sand. They probably don't have as much of a problem with that at the zoo.

Uncle Mark: They probably don't have to sneeze as much either. *(Laughing again.)*

Aunt Trish: *(rolling her eyes)* You and your jokes. Everyone, you will have to excuse my new husband.

Alex: That's OK, Aunt Trish. He's actually pretty funny. Did you see elephants at the zoo? We saw African elephants, and they were huge!

Nina: Our tour guide said that the elephants can weigh up to nine tons. That's more than a car! They are the largest animals that live on land, and the second tallest. Only the giraffe is taller.

Dad: I read an article about the elephants at the San Diego Zoo. The exhibit has African and Asian elephants. Asian elephants are slightly shorter and have somewhat smaller ears.

Aunt Trish: It's so interesting to watch an elephant use its trunk. It's almost like an arm and a hand.

Alex: Our guide said that the trunk is a combination of an upper lip and a nose. Its nostrils are located at the trunk's tip, which has flaps that act like fingers.

Nina: The elephants were picking up branches and using them to scratch themselves. They also picked up dirt and threw it on themselves. They were so dirty!

FLUENCY TIP

Pay attention to the directions in parentheses. They can give you clues about how to read that person's line with expression. For example, read Uncle Mark's lines with a little laugh in your voice.

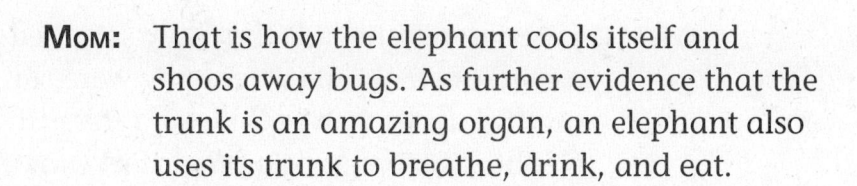

Mom: That is how the elephant cools itself and shoos away bugs. As further evidence that the trunk is an amazing organ, an elephant also uses its trunk to breathe, drink, and eat.

Uncle Mark: *(chuckling)* The elephants at the zoo were not playing an organ. Do you think they wash their trunk before using it to eat or drink?

Dad: I can't say that for sure, but the elephant inhales water with its trunk and then sprays it on itself for a shower. The trunk of an adult elephant can hold about one and a half gallons of water!

Aunt Trish: Some of the elephants we saw at the zoo had large tusks, and some did not.

Uncle Mark: Maybe the elephants without tusks didn't brush their teeth, so they lost them. See what can happen, kids?

Nina: Oh, Uncle Mark, that's not true. Those elephants without tusks were probably female Asian elephants. They don't usually have tusks.

Alex: The African elephants we saw were using their tusks to strip bark from the trees to eat. Our guide told us that the tusks also protect the trunk.

> **FLUENCY TIP**
>
> When you have several lines together, practice reading the words correctly. Then make sure you pause in the right places.

Mom: I used to tell the kids that they sounded like a herd of elephants when they were running around upstairs. Now I know differently, as elephants have pads on their feet that allow them to walk or run with very little noise.

Dad: I wish the kids had pads on their feet, too, but I'm glad their feet aren't as large as an elephant's! Did you know that an elephant's feet expand under its weight and contract when the leg is lifted? This enables them to get out of mud easily.

Uncle Mark: I could have used that adaptation when I was camping last weekend.

Aunt Trish: Finally, you said something almost serious! Your jokes are getting out of hand, honey.

Nina: We saw a lot of camels in Africa, too. They looked so dirty and ragged. Their fur was hanging off them.

Alex: I used to think that camels stored food and water in their hump, kind of like a lunchbox. *(He laughs.)* But that's not true.

Mom: The hump is like a lunchbox, but you won't find food in its original form there. The camel's body changes some of the food it eats into fat and stores the fat in the camel's hump. When food is scarce, the camel gets energy from the stored fat.

Nina: I think it's so cool how camels can walk on sand while carrying such a heavy load.

Uncle Mark: The camels at the zoo were wearing what looked like little cages over their mouth.

AUNT TRISH: It made them look kind of scary. What are those used for?

DAD: That is called a muzzle. A camel has an extremely large mouth with 34 teeth that are strong and sharp. It can use its teeth as weapons, so the zookeepers fasten muzzles on their camels as a **precaution**.

NINA: The hair protects their ears from dust and sand, just like their eyelashes protect their eyes.

AUNT TRISH: They have the most beautiful long, curly eyelashes!

(Dad, Uncle Mark, and Alex roll their eyes.)

MOM: Special **glands** next to the camel's eyes supply water to keep them moist.

✻ **ALEX:** Remember what the guide told us about the camel's diet? I would much rather be eating a cheeseburger.

NINA: Yes, camels have adapted to the desert by eating things that other animals won't, such as thorns and dry leaves. Yuck!

DAD: That's exactly why I like to eat liver and onions. I know that no one will fight me for it. *(Everyone wrinkles his or her nose.)* And I think I do a pretty good job of storing some fat for later, too.

> ✻ **FLUENCY TIP**
>
> In Alex's line, "I would much rather be eating a cheeseburger," stress the word *cheeseburger* with your voice to help you read with more expression.

Mom: *(laughing)* So are you trying to tell us that you are part camel? Does that mean we have to change our habitat, or will you be able to adapt?

Aunt Trish: The camels at the zoo were not eating thorns and dry leaves. There really is a difference, isn't there?

Uncle Mark: Well, they weren't ordering in pizza, either. The zoo gives the animals a good home while trying to make it seem like they are still in the wild. We really learned a lot about the animals that we saw at the zoo.

Nina: I guess we wouldn't be able to see all of the animals if they weren't at the zoo. Not everyone gets a chance to go to other parts of the world to see them in their natural habitats.

Dad: I, for one, would love to visit more countries to observe animals in their natural environments.

Mom, Alex, Nina, and Aunt Trish:
(in unison) I'm with you!

Name _____   Date _____

Comprehension

Write your answer to each question on the lines below.

1. Where was the zoo located? _____

2. What is an advantage to seeing animals in a zoo rather than in the wild?
   _____
   _____

3. Name two similarities and two differences between the animals at the zoo and the animals in Africa.
   _____
   _____

4. Why do you think elephants have the ability to walk or run without making much noise? _____
   _____

5. What is one way in which African elephants differ from Asian elephants?
   _____
   _____

6. What was the most interesting fact you learned about how giraffes have adapted to the conditions of their natural habitat?
   _____
   _____

7. Which of Uncle Mark's jokes did you think was most humorous? Why?
   _____
   _____

8. Which of the animals mentioned in the play would you most like to see in the wild? Explain your choice.
   _____
   _____

Name _____ Date _____

Vocabulary

Write the number of a vocabulary word on the line before its meaning.

1. gland   _____ Care taken beforehand

2. adapt   _____ Natural environment of a living thing

3. species   _____ An organ of the body that makes a special substance

4. precaution   _____ A disguise

5. camouflage   _____ A group of living things that share certain characteristics

6. habitat   _____ To change to suit an environment or situation

Extension

1. Discuss this question in a small group: "What are the pros and cons of having animals in a zoo?"

   - Do zoos have strict guidelines to follow for animal care?
   - Would people get to see these animals elsewhere?
   - Do zoos help reduce the number of endangered animals?

2. What kind of education must you have in order to become a zoologist, zookeeper, or animal trainer?

   - Research three major colleges that offer classes in animal care.
   - Make lists of the types of classes that are required, what kinds of degrees are needed, and how long it takes to complete each degree.

Who Calls the Shots?

Summary
"Who Calls the Shots?" is a six-character play about a boy who has a strange daydream due to his worries about being too short.

Meet the Players

Character	Reading Level
Daniel	0.8
Mom	2.0
Pete Pituitary	4.2
Theo Thyroid	4.1
Ali Adrenal	3.5
Dr. Mendoza	4.0

Fluency Focus
Reading with Word Accuracy

Comprehension Focus
Building Background

Vocabulary
bloodstream
genes
heredity
hormones
metabolism
network
unique

Set the Stage

Teacher Read Aloud *pages 53–54*
This selection is about the heart and how it works. Read the selection aloud, modeling good fluency by pronouncing each word clearly and accurately.

Get Ready

Vocabulary *page 55*
Use this page to introduce important vocabulary. Discuss the Word Play feature, encouraging students to be creative in their responses.

Fluency and Comprehension Warm-Ups *pages 56–57*
Review these pages with students. Use the following for students who need additional help with the concepts:

- **Reading with Word Accuracy** When you come to an unfamiliar word, remember to look for parts of the word that you know. Put the parts together to say a word that makes sense. Then practice saying the word. Try doing this with words from the Read Aloud, such as *nutrients* and *digested*.

- **Building Background** Thinking about what you already know about a topic helps you understand what you read. List at least three things you already know about the heart or the bloodstream. Underline one fact that helps you understand what the Read Aloud is about. What reference books and Internet resources could you use to find more information?

Read Aloud Tip
Introduce the fluency focus of **reading with word accuracy**. Write *contraction* and *simultaneously* on the board. Point out that good readers think about how to pronounce difficult words. They look at each part of the word and then put the parts together. Have students read each word with you, first stressing the separate syllables and then reading the whole word aloud.

Who Calls the Shots? *pages 58–67*

Independent Practice
Set up the groups and assign each student a part. Then have students read through their assigned parts once before small group practice begins.

Small Group Practice
Assemble the groups. You may want to use the following rehearsal schedule. Each rehearsal, which should involve a complete oral read-through, has an activity to guide students.

1. **First Rehearsal:** Students will read together as a group for the first time. Remind them to preview the play for difficult words to practice ahead of time and to reread sentences that don't make sense.

2. **Vocabulary Rehearsal:** Before this rehearsal, have students locate and list the vocabulary words used in the play. Ask group members to turn back to page 55 and alternate reading aloud the definitions for the listed words.

3. **Fluency Rehearsal: Reading with Word Accuracy** Draw students' attention to the word *enlighten* on page 61 of the play. Point out that the word is made up of a prefix (*en-*), a root word (*light*), and a suffix (*-en*). Model pronouncing the prefix, root, and suffix and then blending them together. Have students locate and read aloud additional words with prefixes or suffixes on page 61. (*mighty, bigger, located, divided, produces, longer, thicker*)

4. **Comprehension Rehearsal: Building Background** After this rehearsal, have students work in groups to create T-Charts to record what they know about the endocrine system and what they want to find out. Use the T-Chart on page 10.

5. **Final Rehearsal:** Observe this rehearsal, focusing on students' ability to read with word accuracy. For example, does the student reading the part of Ali Adrenal pronounce the prefix, root, and suffix in the word *triangular* on page 64?

Performance
This is your opportunity to sit back, relax, and enjoy the performance. Encourage students to have fun while performing!

Curtain Call *pages 68–69*
Assign these questions and activities for students to complete either independently or in a group.

Vocabulary Tip
For more vocabulary practice, have students discuss the following:

- What characteristics do you possess that are probably due to **heredity**?
- What might be the result of the body not producing enough growth **hormone**?
- How does what you eat relate to your **bloodstream**?

Who Calls the Shots?

Set the Stage
Teacher Read Aloud

Press the side of your neck, and you'll feel something throbbing just beneath your skin. It's your pulse, or heartbeat. Each beat is caused by the contraction, or squeezing, of your heart. You can measure your heart rate by counting how many beats you feel in one minute—probably between seventy and one hundred.

What happens when you run around the block? You feel your heart pounding in your chest. That's your heart doing its job—beating faster to supply the additional oxygen your body craves. Try running in place and then taking your pulse. Now how many beats do you count in a minute? During an average lifetime, your heart will beat about 2.5 billion times, sending blood to cells in your body. That's quite a job for an organ that's about the size of your clenched fist!

When you think of your heart, you probably conjure up pictures of frilly valentines and red-hot heart candies. Maybe you imagine the broken hearts of love songs. But your heart is actually a pear-shaped muscle located a little to the left of the middle of your chest.

Your heart muscle is made up of two powerful pumps, working side by side. The right pump receives blood from your body and pumps it to your lungs, where it picks up oxygen. Simultaneously, the left pump receives oxygen-rich blood back from your lungs and sends it out to your body.

Whether moving to or from your heart, your blood circulates through an extraordinary network of blood vessels over 60,000 miles long! While thicker-walled vessels, called arteries, rush blood to your body tissues, thinner-walled vessels, called veins, gently drain the blood back to your heart.

Why is this process essential to your life? Your arteries provide your tissues with a constant supply of blood—blood that carries oxygen from your lungs, nutrients from your digested food, and hormones from your glands to cells in your body. Your veins carry carbon dioxide away from your body tissues back to your lungs. It's as though your arteries feed your cells a healthy, hearty meal and your veins are left to take out the garbage! It's a matter of survival.

In this play, you will learn more about your bloodstream and other inner workings of your body. Use the vocabulary and warm-ups on the next three pages to help you get ready to read.

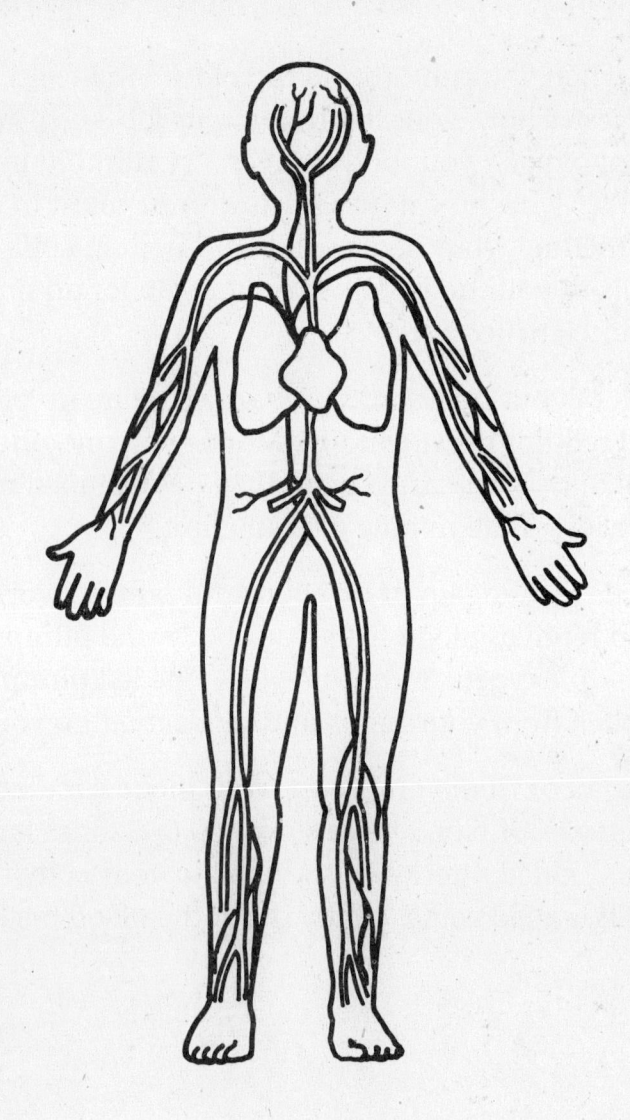

Get Ready

Vocabulary

Read and review these words to prepare for reading the play.

bloodstream, *n.*: the blood as it flows through the body

genes, *n.*: substances in a cell that control the characteristics inherited from parents

heredity, *n.*: the passing of physical or mental characteristics from parents to children

hormones, *n.*: substances formed in the body that affect the way a person grows and develops

metabolism, *n.*: the chemical changes in living cells that provide energy

network, *n.*: a group of things that work together as a unit or system

unique, *adj.*: one of a kind

WORD PLAY

For more vocabulary practice, discuss the following with a partner or in a group:

- Which is more important in winning a marathon—good **genes** or practice?
- What other kinds of **networks** do you know about?
- What makes you **unique**?

Get Ready

Fluency Warm-Up

Reading with Word Accuracy

Fluent readers read with **accuracy**. They learn how to pronounce difficult words, and they learn what the words mean. They do not skip or add words.

Remember to sound out each word as you read and to think about whether your reading makes sense. Use a dictionary to learn about words you don't know.

FLUENCY PRACTICE

Each sentence below contains a mistake. Read the sentences aloud. What word would you change, add, or remove so each sentence makes sense? Write the sentence correctly.

1. The correct tine is 6:30. _____
   _____

2. My books are lined up neatly on shelf. _____
   _____

3. The carpet feels soft beneath my the feet. _____
   _____

4. What's the nest thing you have to do? _____
   _____

Get Ready

Comprehension Warm-Up

Building Background

When fluent readers **build background**, they make connections between what they read and what they know. Sometimes the text reminds them of a personal experience they've had. Sometimes it reminds them of other things they've read. Or it might make them think of something they already know about the world. When readers make these connections, it helps them understand what they read.

You can build background before you read by looking at the pictures in a book. You can read the dust jacket, contents page, or back of the book to learn about what's inside. Before you begin reading, think about what you already know about the topic.

COMPREHENSION TIP

You can build background by asking yourself questions like these.

- Has something similar happened to me?
- Have I ever read about something like this?
- What do I know about this topic, and what do I want to learn?

Readers' Theater

Presents
Who Calls the Shots?
by
Carol Beth Hindin

Cast
(in order of appearance)

Daniel　　　　＿＿＿＿＿＿＿＿＿＿＿＿＿＿＿＿＿＿＿＿

Mom　　　　　＿＿＿＿＿＿＿＿＿＿＿＿＿＿＿＿＿＿＿＿

Pete Pituitary　＿＿＿＿＿＿＿＿＿＿＿＿＿＿＿＿＿＿＿＿

Theo Thyroid　＿＿＿＿＿＿＿＿＿＿＿＿＿＿＿＿＿＿＿＿

Ali Adrenal　　＿＿＿＿＿＿＿＿＿＿＿＿＿＿＿＿＿＿＿＿

Dr. Mendoza　＿＿＿＿＿＿＿＿＿＿＿＿＿＿＿＿＿＿＿＿

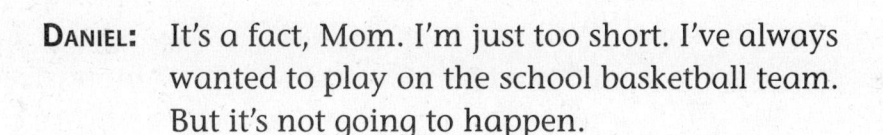

DANIEL: It's a fact, Mom. I'm just too short. I've always wanted to play on the school basketball team. But it's not going to happen.

MOM: Honey, I don't think that's true. You're a good player, and the team needs you. Give it your best shot, and you'll see what happens.

DANIEL: I wish I could grow five inches by Monday's tryouts. That would sure help.

MOM: Daniel, your body will grow when it is ready. I grew a lot in seventh grade. Dad had his growth spurt in eighth grade. You'll just have to wait.

DANIEL: Sure, Mom. That's easy for you to say.

MOM: Dinner is in 15 minutes. And I have a surprise for you. Now go upstairs and wash your hands.

(As Daniel washes his hands, he looks into space and begins to daydream.)

DANIEL: What am I going to do now?

PETE PITUITARY: May I help you, Daniel?

DANIEL: *(shocked by Pete's sudden appearance)* Who are you? Where did you come from?

PETE PITUITARY: Have you ever heard of the endocrine system?

DANIEL: No, I can't say that I have.

Pete Pituitary: Well, my name is Pete. I'm captain for a team of glands that works with your **bloodstream** to make up your endocrine system. We control your energy, your responses to the world, and your growth. I'm happy to take you on a guided tour and introduce you to my teammates.

Daniel: I'm sure glad to meet you! Maybe you can help me grow five inches by Monday! *(Stunned to see his mother in his daydream.)* Wow, Mom! You're here, too! Can you believe this guy?

Mom: I think Pete can teach us both a lot. We just have to listen.

Pete Pituitary: OK, here we go. Your endocrine system is a **network** of glands and organs that has three basic jobs. First my teammates and I produce the **hormones** your body requires. Then we store the hormones until your body needs them. Finally we release them into your bloodstream, where the hormones are transported to your tissues and organs.

Daniel: Let me make sure I have this right. My endocrine system makes hormones. Next it stores them for me. Then it sends the hormones to the places that need them.

Pete Pituitary: You've got it, Daniel! Now, if I'm correct, you are especially interested in one particular hormone, the growth hormone. We like to call it GH.

Daniel: That would be the one, Pete! I need all the GH I can get! Can you send some into my bloodstream before Monday?

MOM: Daniel, let Pete speak. He has a lot to teach us. Pete, I've heard of the growth hormone. But how does it work?

PETE PITUITARY: Stick with me, and I'll enlighten you. As I said before, I'm the guy in charge. I'm your pituitary gland—tiny, but mighty. I'm no bigger than a pea, and I'm located at the base of your brain.

MOM: Do you make GH?

✻ **PETE PITUITARY:** Yes, I do. I'm divided into two parts—the anterior, or front part, and the posterior, or back part. My anterior part produces GH, which stimulates growth during childhood, making your bones grow longer and thicker.

DANIEL: Can your front part make some more GH for me?

PETE PITUITARY: I know I said I'm the guy in charge. However, I do depend on other glands in our endocrine system. Let me introduce you to my pal Theo Thyroid.

THEO THYROID: Hi, folks. I'm your thyroid gland. I'm larger than my friend Pete, and I lie on both sides of your trachea. Your trachea is the breathing airway in your neck. A thin strip of tissue connects my two parts, so I look like the letter *H*. Just think *handsome* or *hero*. That's me!

> ✻ **FLUENCY TIP**
>
> Be sure you read the words *anterior* (an TEER ee er) and *posterior* (pa STEER ee er) with no mistakes.

Pete Pituitary: OK, Theo. We all agree that you're one terrific guy. Now tell Daniel and his mom what you do for a living.

Theo Thyroid: I produce the thyroid hormones that regulate your **metabolism**. That means I'm responsible for everything that goes on in your body to keep you alive and growing—like breathing, digesting your food, and keeping your blood moving.

Mom: Daniel, do you remember my Aunt Lily? Her body didn't make enough thyroid hormone. So she always felt very weak. Then her doctor gave her thyroid pills. Now she feels much stronger.

Theo Thyroid: I'm glad the doctor was able to help Aunt Lily with her thyroid problem. Children can have the same problem, though it's rare. When they don't have enough thyroid hormone, children grow more slowly. They don't reach their full height.

Daniel: Theo, did you say "grow more slowly"? That's it! That's the answer. I need more thyroid hormone, just like Aunt Lily. Can you get me some by Monday?

Mom: That's not the answer, Daniel. Last week, Dr. Mendoza checked your blood. All your hormone levels were just fine. You do not have a thyroid problem. You are a healthy, growing boy.

Pete Pituitary: She's right, Daniel. Theo and I have done our jobs well. We've supplied you with the correct amounts of growth and thyroid hormones.

Theo Thyroid: Our little chat seems to be drawing to a close. So I would like to take just a moment to thank you for your visit. I would also like to suggest you check out my friend Ali Adrenal. Her work may be of interest to you. Happy travels.

✻ Daniel: This tour has not helped me one bit. I'm not any taller, but I sure am hungrier. Mom, is dinner almost ready?

Mom: Yes, Daniel. Dinner will be on the table soon. However, I'd like to continue our tour. We both have a lot to learn from Pete and Theo.

Pete Pituitary: Well, thank you for your vote of confidence. At this point, I suggest we follow Theo's advice and visit Ali Adrenal. Let's make our way down to the kidneys and see what Ali's up to today. *(To Theo.)* Theo, why don't you join us? *(To Daniel and Mom.)* We'll lead, and you follow.

Daniel: Do I have a choice? Never mind. I know the answer. Let's move on. I'll just keep thinking about yummy hamburgers for dinner.

Theo Thyroid: Now I'd like to introduce you to Ali Adrenal. Ali, this is Daniel and his mom. Pete and I are acting as their tour guides today.

> **✻ FLUENCY TIP**
>
> When you read the part where Daniel asks his mom if dinner is ready, be sure to say *hungrier* instead of *hungry*. Read carefully so you don't say the wrong word.

Ali Adrenal: It's nice to meet you both. I don't get out much, and I love to see new faces. It makes life so much more interesting.

Pete Pituitary: Ali, please explain your daily functions. We're all ears. Well, we're really not. Some of us are glands, and some of us are humans. But we're all listening.

Ali Adrenal: First I would like to welcome you to my home. Two homes, really. I have two lovely, triangular homes—one on top of each kidney.

Mom: Ali, thank you for having us. I hope we are not in your way.

Ali Adrenal: You're no problem at all. Now let me tell you what we do. As I said, I have two triangular homes. In my homes, we produce hormones that help you handle the stress of illness and injury. When you're sick, we help you regain your strength. We're the ones who get you on your feet and back to school lickety-split.

Daniel: Gee, thanks, Ali.

Ali Adrenal: You're welcome, Daniel. And that's not all. We also help you with the other stresses in your life. We're there for you when you're sweating over your difficult test. And we come to your rescue when you find yourself face-to-face with a tiger.

Daniel: I can't say that I've come across any tigers lately.

> **FLUENCY TIP**
>
> Ali's parts are long. When you read them, don't leave any words out. Read each word correctly.

ALI ADRENAL: Well, how about this? We can help you cope with the stress of sixth-grade basketball tryouts.

DANIEL: Can you stop by next Monday at 3:00?

ALI ADRENAL: We'll be at your school gym, cheering you on. Just look for us in the bleachers, Daniel. We'll be wearing red hats shaped like triangles.

THEO THYROID: Ali, explain to Daniel and his mom how you and I work as a team.

ALI ADRENAL: Sure. My adrenal glands and Theo's thyroid gland work together to regulate your metabolism. We help your body change food into energy.

MOM: *(outside the daydream, calling upstairs)* Daniel, who are you talking to? Oh, never mind. Your hamburger is ready. And I still have that surprise I promised.

DANIEL: *(takes his place at the dinner table)* Thanks, Mom. Yum, hamburgers. What's my surprise?

MOM: *(as the doorbell rings)* There's your surprise right now, honey. *(Mom shows Dr. Mendoza to the table.)* Welcome, Dr. Mendoza. We're so glad you could join us for dinner.

DR. MENDOZA: Thanks for your hospitality. It's a pleasure to see you both again. Daniel, you've grown since your last checkup. I hardly recognize you.

DANIEL: I'm glad you're here, Dr. Mendoza. I have some questions . . .

MOM: Oh, Daniel. Let Dr. Mendoza enjoy dinner.

Dr. Mendoza: I appreciate your concern, but I'm delighted to answer any questions Daniel might have. What seems to be troubling you, young man?

Daniel: Well, I guess I should just say it. Why am I so short?

Dr. Mendoza: Daniel, I'm glad you asked. However, you should realize that you are not so short. At this moment, you are precisely the correct height for you.

Daniel: Huh?

Dr. Mendoza: Let me explain. Daniel, I have kept track of your height since the day you were born. In fact, I have maintained a chart that shows your growth over the last 11 years. When I look at your chart, I observe a consistent growth curve. In other words, I see a steady increase in your height over your lifetime. You are a normal, healthy, growing boy.

Mom: That's what I keep telling you, Daniel.

Daniel: I'm shorter than the other boys in my class. I may be healthy, but I'm still short.

Dr. Mendoza: I acknowledge your concern. All I can do is reassure you that every individual has a **unique** pattern of growth. Who's your best friend, Daniel?

Daniel: Alex. And Alex is taller than I am!

Dr. Mendoza: Have you ever been taller than Alex?

Daniel: Yeah. When we were in third grade, I was taller. I could make jump balls that Alex couldn't make!

Dr. Mendoza: That's precisely what I mean. You and Alex have your own unique growth patterns, so you each grow at your own rate. If you both maintain your health, then each of you will reach the height you were meant to be.

Daniel: Well, maybe I'm meant to be short.

Dr. Mendoza: Maybe you are, and maybe you're not. We'll have to wait and see. Your height depends on hormones, **heredity**, and nutrition.

Mom: Let's talk about heredity now. Can you tell Daniel how heredity might affect his height?

Dr. Mendoza: Sure. The **genes** you inherit from your parents determine many of the characteristics you see when you look in the mirror. They are responsible for your dark brown hair and eyes, your short nose, and your full lips. These genes also affect your final height.

Daniel: So that's that. I can't change my genes.

Dr. Mendoza: True. However, you can do something about your nutrition. When you consume healthful foods, you increase your ability to grow.

✶ **Daniel:** Thanks, Dr. Mendoza. I'll eat my green beans today. I'll give it my best shot on Monday. And someday I'll see how tall I'm supposed to be!

> ✶ **FLUENCY TIP**
>
> When you read Daniel's last lines, don't say *I* instead of *I'll*. Don't say the wrong word.

Name _____   Date _____

Comprehension

Write your answer to each question on the lines below.

1. What is Daniel concerned about at the beginning of the play?
   _____
   _____

2. Which character refers to himself as the captain of the endocrine "team"?
   _____
   _____

3. What is the endocrine system and what does it do?
   _____
   _____

4. What three factors can influence your height?
   _____
   _____

5. Does Daniel need help from his doctor to grow properly?
   _____
   _____

6. Will Daniel's hamburger help him grow? Why or why not?
   _____
   _____

7. What does Daniel learn about his own growth and development?
   _____
   _____

8. Have you ever had a problem like Daniel's? Explain.
   _____
   _____

Name _____ Date _____

Vocabulary

Write the number of a vocabulary word on the line before its meaning.

1. heredity   _____ Group of things working together as a system
2. network   _____ Substances that control heredity
3. unique   _____ System of blood flowing through the body
4. genes   _____ Passing of physical characteristics from parents to children
5. metabolism   _____ One of a kind
6. hormones   _____ Process of chemical change that provides energy for the body
7. bloodstream   _____ Substances that affect the body's growth and development

Extension

1. Discuss this question in a small group: "What might happen if people could choose their own height and weight?"
   - How would people make these choices?
   - How would this affect the world of sports?
   - How would this affect everyday life?

2. Write your own travel fantasy about a place you've always wanted to explore. Then read your fantasy to the class.
   - Where will you go? Why?
   - Who will you meet?
   - What experiences will you have?
   - What will you learn?

The Mummy's Curse

Summary
"The Mummy's Curse" is a six-character play about a family visiting an Egyptian tomb and making an amazing discovery.

Meet the Players

Character	Reading Level
Jenna	2.6
Colin	1.9
Ben	2.9
Mom	2.3
Dad	3.1
Anwar	4.4

Fluency Focus
Proper Phrasing

Comprehension Focus
Asking Questions

Vocabulary
archaeologist
balcony
graffiti
hieroglyphics
mummy
tomb
vile

Set the Stage

Teacher Read Aloud pages 72–73
This selection is about Egypt's mysterious Sphinx. Ask students to listen carefully to the phrasing as you read the selection aloud.

Get Ready

Vocabulary page 74
Use this page to introduce important vocabulary. Discuss the Word Play feature, encouraging students to be creative in their responses.

Fluency and Comprehension Warm-Ups pages 75–76
Review these pages with students. Use the following for students who need additional help with the concepts:

- **Proper Phrasing** Look at the second sentence in paragraph 5 of the Read Aloud. Listen to one way of phrasing the sentence: *Early attempts included—adding cement to—firm up—the limestone.* Now listen to a different way of phrasing: *Early attempts—included adding cement—to firm up the limestone.* Which phrasing is easier to understand?

- **Asking Questions** Before reading, good readers ask themselves what they already know about a topic. During reading, they ask what might happen next. After reading, they ask, "What did I learn?" As you look at the Read Aloud, put a self-stick note next to one sentence that answers the question "What did I learn about the Sphinx?"

Read Aloud Tip
Explain that the fluency focus of **proper phrasing** involves reading in phrases, or chunks, rather than one word at a time. Point out that in the second sentence in the Read Aloud, the phrases are separated by commas. Read the sentence twice, first stressing the phrase boundaries by pausing longer than normal and then modeling how to read the phrase smoothly in sequence.

The Mummy's Curse pages 77–86

Independent Practice
Set up the groups and assign each student a part. Then have students read through their assigned parts once before small group practice begins.

Small Group Practice
Assemble the groups. You may want to use the following rehearsal schedule. Each rehearsal, which should involve a complete oral read-through, has an activity to guide students.

1. First Rehearsal: Point out that this play includes many stage directions. Invite students to locate and practice a stage direction for their characters. Then ask students to read together for the first time.

2. Vocabulary Rehearsal: Encourage students to locate the vocabulary words in the play. Then challenge each student to compose a sentence that includes two vocabulary words, such as "The *archaeologist* found six *mummies*." Have students share their sentences with partners.

3. Fluency Rehearsal: Proper Phrasing Have students review page 75. Then for the rehearsal, designate one student to be the tip reader. At the ends of pages 79, 84, and 86, ask the tip reader to read the tip aloud. After the reading, have volunteers choose one tip and model using it as a guide for reading a line of the play.

4. Comprehension Rehearsal: Asking Questions During this rehearsal, have students work in their groups to answer this question: What are we supposed to learn from this play? Ask them to list at least three facts or ideas they think the author wanted to teach through the play.

5. Final Rehearsal: Observe this rehearsal, focusing on students' phrasing. For example, on page 79 of the play, note whether the student reading Dad's part uses the ellipses as a signal to chunk the words in an unusual and dramatic way by pausing before announcing what the family is going to be doing.

Performance
This is your opportunity to sit back, relax, and enjoy the performance. Encourage students to have fun while performing!

Curtain Call pages 87–88
Assign these questions and activities for students to complete either independently or in a group.

Vocabulary Tip
For more vocabulary practice, have students discuss the following:
- Why do you think some people put **graffiti** on walls in public places?
- How is a **tomb** different from a gravestone?
- Where might you see a **balcony**?

The Mummy's Curse

Set the Stage
Teacher Read Aloud

Have you ever heard of the Great Sphinx? The Sphinx, one of the most famous monuments in Egypt, is a limestone statue with the head of a pharaoh and the body of a lion. The head is thought to be a royal portrait of King Khafre, since his pyramid is behind the Sphinx, at the site of the famous Giza pyramids. Some believe the purpose of the Sphinx was to be a guardian spirit for Khafre's burial area. The Sphinx is enormous. It measures 187 feet long and 66 feet high. The face is 20 feet wide.

Many books and articles explore the mysteries of the Sphinx. One mystery concerns the Sphinx's nose, which has been missing for some time. The popular story is that Napoleon Bonaparte's troops shot off the nose during target practice in 1798. However, drawings made before 1798 show the Sphinx without a nose.

Another mystery involves secret chambers inside the Sphinx. In the 1930s, excavators documented tunnels and open areas inside the Sphinx. Some think that the Sphinx is an unfinished tomb. Some think that more tunnels may be discovered.

Although drifting sand covered the Sphinx for much of its 4,600 years, wind and water have eroded its unprotected areas. One Egyptologist has called the erosion a "cancer." But erosion is not entirely to blame for the condition of the statue. Other sources have damaged the Sphinx since excavators uncovered it in the 1930s. Vibrations from air and vehicle traffic, blasting at nearby quarries, air pollution, and lighting for tourists have all contributed to the problem.

Since the first recorded restoration in 1400 B.C., many have tried to preserve the Sphinx. Early attempts included adding cement to firm up the limestone. However, that only slowed the outside deterioration—the deterioration continued under the cement. More recently, in the 1980s, workers began a restoration project using lime and sand mortar. Upon the completion of this ten-year project in 1998, Egyptian President Hosni Mubarak announced to the world that the Sphinx was safe from further damage. Another dignitary declared that the Sphinx would live on "as a symbol of life and a witness to history."

There are other sphinx monuments in Egypt. The others have lion bodies, but some have ram heads or hawk heads. The Greeks also have sphinx monuments. However, those monuments have the body of a lion, the head of a woman, and wings.

Some believe many more monuments will be found in Egypt. The sand may hide many more secrets. Those monuments already revealed will surely need vigilant effort to be maintained. The Sphinx, as an emblem of Egypt and a priceless piece of ancient Egyptian heritage, will need human help in order to endure.

In this play, you will learn more about ancient Egypt. Along the way, you will practice your reading. Use the vocabulary and warm-ups on the next three pages to get ready to read.

Get Ready

Vocabulary

Read and review these words to prepare for reading the play.

archaeologist, *n.*: an expert who learns about life in ancient times by finding and studying the objects left behind

balcony, *n.*: a platform with a railing on an upper floor of a building

graffiti, *n.*: drawings or writing done on a wall or other surface

hieroglyphics, *n.*: ancient picture writing

mummy, *n.*: a dried and preserved dead body

tomb, *n.*: place of burial

vile, *adj.*: disgusting, foul

WORD PLAY

For more vocabulary practice, discuss the following with a partner or in a group.

- What kinds of objects might **archaeologists** study?
- Design your own **hieroglyph** to symbolize you. On a sheet of paper, draw four to six appropriate pictures or symbols that say something about who you are and what you like. Then tell your partner about what you drew.
- Are some of your chores **vile**? Which ones?

Get Ready

Fluency Warm-Up

Proper Phrasing

To be a fluent reader, you need to read sentences in chunks, or **phrases**, instead of stopping after each word. This will help you read more smoothly and better understand what you read.

YOU NEED / TO READ / IN CHUNKS

Often, punctuation will help you phrase correctly. However, sometimes you'll have to figure out the phrasing on your own. The key is grouping words that look and sound like they go together.

FLUENCY PRACTICE

Rewrite the sentences below, putting a slash between each natural-sounding phrase. Try to break each sentence into three or four phrases. Example: Good readers / look ahead / for words / that go together.

1. Our friendly neighbors are planning a neighborhood picnic for this weekend.
2. Surprised at her luck, Amy got a glimpse of her favorite star walking down the red carpet.
3. I'm trying to do more volunteer work because it makes me feel good inside.

Get Ready

Comprehension Warm-Up

Asking Questions

Good readers pause to **ask questions**. Then they search for the answers. Asking questions helps them focus on what they are reading. It helps them clarify when something in the text seems confusing. It also helps them think more deeply about what they are reading.

Ask yourself questions to help you understand what you read. Keep track of the questions you ask yourself. Try using self-stick notes or a journal. Then make sure to find those answers!

COMPREHENSION TIP

Stop and ask yourself questions like these as you read.

- What is this about?
- What questions do I have at this point?
- What does the author want me to know?
- Do any words look important?
- Can I relate this to my own experience?

Readers' Theater

Presents
The Mummy's Curse
by
Laura Layton Strom

Cast
(in order of appearance)

Jenna _____

Colin _____

Ben _____

Mom _____

Dad _____

Anwar _____

JENNA: Before we start this story, let's get something straight. I get plane sick, train sick, and car sick. I really don't like to go anywhere, and I don't like the heat or dark places. So when my parents said we had to go to Egypt, I was not at all happy. But being 14, I can't stay home alone. So off to Egypt I went, with a barf bag and a carry-on bag.

COLIN: Let me say something, too. My sister is such a bother.

JENNA: Hey!

COLIN: I call them like I see them. Anyway, I'm 10 and I'm happy about the Egypt trip. We just arrived this morning. The flight wasn't bad. I got to play video games for 18 hours. No one told me to take out the trash or walk the dog. Flying is excellent!

BEN: Is it my turn to talk? Well, I'm Ben and I'm 12. I love everything about Egypt. Let me give you some background. Egypt is in the northeast corner of Africa. The ancient Egyptian civilization started about 3000 B.C. *(Pauses.)*

(Jenna makes snoring sound.)

BEN: *(ignoring her)* Ancient Egypt is famous for its pyramids and **mummies**, among other things. Mummies are just the coolest. I've watched every show on mummies. My goal for this trip is to see a mummy, live and in person.

JENNA: *(sarcastic)* Mummies are DEAD, Ben! Don't be absurd.

BEN: (sarcastic) It's a figure of speech, Jenna!

JENNA: Whatever. My goal for the trip is to wallow in misery and catch up on my sleep.

MOM: Hey, kids. What are you doing?

✻ **JENNA, COLIN, BEN:** (in unison) Nothing.

MOM: Well, we're getting the jeep ready. So, get your backpacks and fill your water bottles. We're going to explore!

JENNA: Just what are we exploring, anyway? I'd like to explore the inside of my eyelids while I sunbathe on the **balcony**.

DAD: Hold on to your hats, kids. We are . . . visiting a pharaoh's **tomb**! My friend Anwar is taking us. He is the leader of a dig.

BEN: Are there mummies? I think I could be a great mummy detective. I will do anything to search out a real, honest-to-goodness mummy.

MOM: Hmmm. They haven't found mummies. They have uncovered walls painted with picture writing.

JENNA: Thrilling. Some old guy leaves **graffiti** on a wall, and we have to spend a whole day looking at it.

COLIN: It does sound kind of boring, Mom. I don't want to spend my vacation looking at walls.

> ✻ **FLUENCY TIP**
>
> People sometimes speak in incomplete sentences. See above for the line "Nothing." Always stop at end punctuation, even if it marks an incomplete sentence.

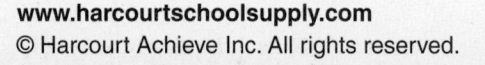

Mom: Oh, don't be silly. This will be more interesting than sleeping or video games. This is real life and real history. We will take a peek into the past. And maybe we will see something really cool.

Ben: Like mummies? Or jars of their organs?

Mom: No promises. But where there is a tomb, there might be a mummy.

(The family and Anwar, their guide, arrive near the tomb.)

Anwar: I'm going to park the jeep here, because we can't drive near the site. We'll take camels from here; it's just a short ride.

Jenna: Did someone utter the word *camels*?

Colin: Awesome! I can't wait to tell my friends I rode a camel!

Dad: I told you that getting there is half the fun! Maybe, though, I should tell you a few things about camels first. Camels are a very special animal. They can go for days without water. Some people think camels store water in their hump. But actually they conserve water in their body cells and stomach. And camels are fast drinkers when they find some water. In fact, when they drink, they can absorb 25 gallons of water in 5 to 10 minutes. But beware. Camels can have a temper. They've been known to huff and spit.

Jenna: *(alarmed about her camel)* Mom! It's all dirty, and it smells **vile**. What if it spits on me?

Mom: You'll be fine. Where's your sense of adventure?

(All arrive at tomb site.)

ANWAR: Before we go in, let me tell you a few things to caution you. Ancient Egyptian legends say that a curse was put on each tomb as it was sealed. Many believe the legends were made up to scare away potential robbers. But many others believe the curses to be true. Oddly, bad things have happened to people who have broken into tombs. Coincidence or curse—who is to say?

COLIN: Wow! I bet those robbers are sorry now. So just what has happened to people?

ANWAR: Ah, so you want details. Have you all heard of King Tutankhamen, or King Tut, as many call him?

BEN: Of course we have. King Tut was buried with amazing treasures. His tomb was one of the few that wasn't robbed blind.

ANWAR: Right. King Tut's treasures are amazing, and you can see them at the Egyptian Museum where I work. Some of the treasures have even toured other museums in the world. They are truly breathtaking. But back to the curse. Some people believe there is a Tutankhamen curse. Legend says that threats and warnings of possible death appear in **hieroglyphics** at his tomb's entrances. Some people mysteriously died after opening the tomb. The people who took things out of the tomb seemed to suffer the worst fates. And there is even the story of a pet parakeet swallowed by a cobra right after the bird left Tut's tomb.

Jenna: Now that is the scariest-sounding graffiti I've ever heard of!

Ben: Cool! Horror awaits us!

Colin: So will we see some treasures today? I'd enjoy finding a gold mask or a big ruby!

Jenna: Ruby? Did someone say ruby? Riding this lumpy horse might be worth it if I find a ruby!

Dad: Let's not get carried away. Anwar is a scientist. He is an **archaeologist** for the Egyptian Museum. He doesn't keep what he finds.

Jenna: *(under her breath to the audience)* Yeah, but I'm not an archaeologist.

Anwar: *(with a teasingly wicked smile)* So I just want to apologize up front, in case we become cursed.

(The group enters the tomb.)

Anwar: If you look over here, you'll see where we have uncovered two secret passageways. The tomb builders tried to confuse robbers by creating a main entry that dead-ends. They then built hidden passageways. One of these passageways may end up leading to the burial chamber. The burial chamber may include a mummy and treasures. *(Phone beeps. He answers it. Listens. Responds.)* Yes. Yes. But . . . OK. *(Closes phone and hooks it back on his belt. Talks to group.)* Sorry, but it seems something was found this morning that I urgently need to see. I really shouldn't leave you here alone, but the sun is scorching hot outside. I can't leave you out there.

Dad: That's OK, Anwar. We'll be fine inside.

Anwar: OK, I'll assume you will be fine, and I'll be back as quickly as I can.

Mom: So, guys, let's pull up a rock. Isn't this exciting! We're sitting in a 3,000-year-old tomb. *(Pauses.)* Hey, no wisecrack, Jenna? Jenna? Where's Jenna?

Colin: *(looks from side to side)* Gee, she was here just a minute ago. Maybe she decided to get some sleep after all. She is probably kicking a mummy out of its coffin as we speak.

Mom: Oh, this is not good. One of Anwar's men is still in the hospital. He leaned against a trick wall. He was stuck inside without food or water for four days.

Dad: We'll find her. We just need a plan. *(Speaking to Mom.)* Why don't you take Ben, and I'll take Colin, and we'll each take a passageway. Boys, please gather some pebbles.

Mom: I see. We'll drop pebbles to mark our trail.

Dad: Exactly!

Mom: Let's get our flashlights and get going.

(The teams separate and make their way down the passageways.)

Ben: Hey! Look at this, Mom. *(He picks up something small in the corner.)* This looks like Jenna's red hair clip. Why would it be here . . . ere . . . ere . . . ere. *(Falling through trapdoor.)* Aaaaahhhhh! *(Lands.)* Ugh! *(Pauses.)* Mom! Mom! I fell through a trapdoor. I'm OK. Can you hear me?

Jenna: *(crawling out from behind a corner)* Bravo, Sherlock. You found me. But how do we escape this vile pit?

Ben: *(relieved)* Jenna! I'm so glad you are OK! I mean, Mom was with me, and she saw me fall through the trapdoor. I'm sure she'll get help. In the meantime, we should just sit here and wait.

Jenna: Good idea. Because I was thinking of going on a bike ride, but I'll just sit here and wait.

✷ **Ben:** You should be grateful that someone found you in this underground Tut hut.

Jenna: Thanks for coming down here to provide me with entertainment and to use up the remaining oxygen.

Ben: Oh, you are cheery. We're not going to die. So what is that you are sitting on anyway?

(A cracking sound is heard above, and the teens look up.)

Colin: *(screaming as he falls)* Whoa!!!!! *(Lands on Jenna's lap.)*

Jenna: Oh, man! Another brother falls from the sky. It's raining boys! This is the worst place on Earth.

✷ **FLUENCY TIP**

In Ben's line, pay attention to phrasing: "You should be grateful / that someone found you / in this underground Tut hut."

Colin: Sorry! I was just walking with Dad. All of a sudden I wasn't. Thanks for giving me a soft landing, Jenna. *(Jenna rolls eyes.)* I'm glad you are all right.

Ben: Hey! Do you realize where we are?

Colin: I'm following you. Two trapdoors lead to one place. We are probably in the mummy's bedroom!

Jenna: *(dusting herself off)* Oh, great. We're in the burial chamber. I'm covered in mummy dust and tomb scum!

Colin: Maybe there IS a mummy in here! And maybe some mummy treasures!

(The kids frantically search the chamber. They look high and low. Then a flashlight appears from above.)

Mom: Hey! Anyone down there?

(Later that night at the hotel.)

Dad: Well, that was more adventure than we expected. Jenna, I ought to be really angry at your behavior. But we did make the news tonight, and everyone is OK. I guess that a good scare is a punishment.

Anwar: It is amazing that your random journey turned into the discovery of two ways into the burial chamber.

Ben: Fortunately, I found Jenna's red hair clip. Otherwise, I might not have seen, or felt *(Rubs backside.)* the trapdoor opening.

Anwar: I guess your red hair clip saved the day, Jenna. You didn't get your ruby, but something ruby colored, in the long run, brought you luck.

Jenna: *(secretively to the audience)* Who says I didn't get a ruby! *(Smiles to herself as she looks in her hand. She puts something small into an outside pocket of her suitcase and zips it closed. She rejoins the others.)*

✷ **Colin:** *(steps forward, speaking as a narrator)* Just then, there is a loud clap of thunder. Lightning flashes. It hits the wooden balcony. It catches fire. The fire spreads quickly to the hotel curtains. The group has no time to save anything but themselves. They all run out to safety. Everything in the room is destroyed.

✷ **FLUENCY TIP**

Colin's narrator part should be read very dramatically. Pay attention to phrasing and stress key words. For example, "EVERYTHING / in the ROOM / is DESTROYED."

Name _____   Date _____

Comprehension

Write your answer to each question on the lines below.

1. How is Jenna's reaction to the plans for the trip different from her brothers' reactions?
   _____
   _____

2. Why were there secret passageways and trapdoors in Egyptian tombs?
   _____
   _____

3. What does Jenna hope to find in the tomb?
   _____
   _____

4. Why does the author have Anwar tell the children the scary legends?
   _____
   _____

5. What is significant about the red hair clip?
   _____
   _____

6. Do you think some Egyptian tombs are really cursed? Why or why not?
   _____
   _____

7. Why do you think the story of Jenna's adventure makes the news?
   _____
   _____

8. Why do you think the author has the play end with a fire destroying everything?
   _____
   _____

Name _____   Date _____

Vocabulary

Finish the paragraphs by writing a vocabulary word on each line.

> balcony   tomb   graffiti   vile
> mummy   archaeologist   hieroglyphics

"Ugh!" muttered the (1) _____ as he entered the hotel room at the end of a long day. "What is that (2) _____ smell? The (3) _____ we found in the (4) _____ today is thousands of years old—and it didn't smell *this* bad."

"Relax," said his co-worker. "That's my lunch you smell. I left it out on the (5) _____ all day, and my sandwich spoiled."

Extension

1. Discuss this question in a small group: "Is it OK for people to remove items from tombs?"

    - Who should be allowed to remove items? Who should not?
    - What are good reasons to remove items? What are not?
    - Where should the items be taken after they are removed?

2. What was school like in ancient Egypt? At age 11 or 12, would you be in school if you lived back then? Or would you be expected or forced to do something else?

    - Research education in ancient Egypt.
    - Find out who went to school and for how many years.
    - Make a Venn diagram comparing schools of ancient Egypt to schools today. Use the Venn diagram on page 11.

The Writing Is on the Wall

Summary
"The Writing Is on the Wall" is a six-character play about a class field trip to the Museum of Archaeology.

Meet the Players

Character	Reading Level
Miss Williams	5.2
Jeremy	2.8
Selena	3.1
Colette	6.3
Andre	1.6
Museum Guide	6.7

Fluency Focus
Using Expression

Comprehension Focus
Identifying Main Idea

Vocabulary
archaeologist
decipher
epigrapher
geologist
hieroglyphics
paleontologist
replica
scribe

Set the Stage

Teacher Read Aloud *pages 91–92*
This selection is about ancient hieroglyphic writing and the different peoples that used it. Ask students to listen carefully to your expression as you read the selection aloud.

Get Ready

Vocabulary *page 93*
Use this page to introduce important vocabulary. Discuss the Word Play feature, encouraging students to use specific, concrete details in their responses.

Fluency and Comprehension Warm-Ups *pages 94–95*
Review these pages with students. Use the following for students who need additional help with the concepts:

- **Using Expression** Part of reading with expression is deciding what words to stress, or read with a stronger voice. Read the first sentence of the Read Aloud together, stressing these important words: *writing, ideas, sounds*.

- **Identifying Main Idea** An entire selection has a main idea. Often, so does each paragraph within the selection. Look at paragraph 6 of the Read Aloud. Find and read aloud the sentence that describes the main idea.

Read Aloud Tip
Introduce the fluency focus of **using expression**. Explain that readers make text more interesting by stressing key words. Reread the last sentence in paragraph 1 of the Read Aloud, emphasizing the words *Hittites*, *Maya*, and *Aztec*. Invite students to suggest a word to stress in the next paragraph and then have a volunteer read that sentence aloud.

The Writing Is on the Wall *pages 96–105*

Independent Practice
Set up the groups and assign each student a part. Then have students read through their assigned parts once before small group practice begins.

Small Group Practice
Assemble the groups. You may want to use the following rehearsal schedule. Each rehearsal, which should involve a complete oral read-through, has an activity to guide students.

1. First Rehearsal: Invite students to scan the entire play to find italicized stage directions. Point out that these directions tell actors how to speak or what to do. Then ask students to read together as a group for the first time.

2. Vocabulary Rehearsal: Have students locate the vocabulary words used in the play. As students locate each word, ask them to read in unison the sentence that includes that word. Challenge volunteers to use the words in sentences that explain the words' meaning, such as: "An *archaeologist* is a person who studies ancient cultures."

3. Fluency Rehearsal: Using Expression Review page 94 and the Fluency Tips on pages 98, 101, and 104. Remind students to consider the characters' feelings and to use their voices to express them. After the reading, ask students to work in groups to locate two or three sentences that express excitement or other feelings and to take turns reading them to the group.

4. Comprehension Rehearsal: Identifying Main Idea After this rehearsal, have students work in their groups to create Main Idea Webs. The Main Idea Web should list the main idea of the play in the center and at least six details around the main idea. Use the Main Idea Web on page 12.

5. Final Rehearsal: Observe this rehearsal, focusing on students' expression. For example, for Jeremy's first lines on page 97, note whether the student raises his or her voice at the end of the first sentence and uses an excited tone of voice for the second sentence.

Performance
This is your opportunity to sit back, relax, and enjoy the performance. Encourage students to have fun while performing!

Curtain Call *pages 106–107*
Assign these questions and activities for students to complete either independently or in a group.

Vocabulary Tip

For more vocabulary practice, have students discuss the following:

- How does the work of an **archaeologist** differ from that of a **geologist**?
- Who would be more interested in dinosaurs: an **epigrapher** or a **paleontologist**?

The Writing Is on the Wall

Set the Stage
Teacher Read Aloud

Hieroglyphics is a system of writing that uses picture symbols to represent ideas and sounds. The name *hieroglyphic* comes from the Greek words for "sacred carving." It usually refers to Egyptian writing. However, forms of picture writing were used in other ancient cultures as well. The Hittites had their own form of hieroglyphics, as did the Maya and the Aztec.

The ancient Egyptians used hieroglyphic writing mostly for religious inscriptions on temple walls and stone monuments. Egyptian hieroglyphics included over 700 symbols and grew to contain more than 6,000 symbols by about 300 B.C.

The earliest hieroglyphs, or symbols, consisted of many pictorial characters known as pictographs or ideograms. There were also phonetic hieroglyphs, called phonograms. These phonetic hieroglyphs represented the sounds of the language. The Egyptians wrote phonetic hieroglyphs that represented only the consonants, not the vowels. Because of this, scholars are still unsure of the pronunciation of the ancient Egyptian language.

Some hieroglyphics are read from right to left and others from left to right, depending on the direction the hieroglyphics are facing. Highly trained men called scribes wrote or carved the inscriptions in columns, which were read from top to bottom. Often, hieroglyphs were used as decoration and painted with bright colors or covered with gold.

In Central America, the oldest discovered Maya hieroglyphics date from about A.D. 250. The Maya carved hieroglyphics on buildings and large stone monuments called stelae (STEE lee). These carvings often depicted important events in history in the lives of Maya rulers. The Maya also painted hieroglyphs on pottery and wrote them on paper made from fig tree bark.

The Aztec developed a system of writing that included pictographs used to represent sounds. Aztec writing combined the symbols of many objects to form the sound or name of another object. These symbols are similar to rebus writing.

The Hittites invented a hieroglyphic writing system about 1500 B.C. Some symbols represented words, while others represented sounds.

As writing progressed and became more common, a need developed for a material that was easy to transport and store. The Egyptians used reed plants to make papyrus, a material much like paper. It was easier to write on than stone. Scribes used brushes made of reeds and ink made of soot mixed with water to write on the papyrus.

In this play, you will learn about natural stone monuments and hieroglyphics. Along the way you will also practice your reading. Use the vocabulary and warm-ups on the next three pages to get ready to read.

Get Ready

Vocabulary

Read and review these words to prepare for reading the play.

archaeologist, *n.*: an expert who studies remains from life in ancient times

decipher, *v.*: to translate the signs of a language or writing system

epigrapher (eh PIH gruh fer), *n.*: an expert who studies systems of writing

geologist, *n.*: an expert who studies the history of the earth through rocks

hieroglyphics, *n.*: ancient picture writing

paleontologist (pay lee on TAH luh jist), *n.*: an expert who studies fossil remains

replica, *n.*: an exact copy or model of an original, though sometimes scaled down to a smaller size

scribe, *n.*: a writer or record keeper

WORD PLAY

For more vocabulary practice, discuss the following with a partner or in a group.

- Can you **decipher** what the answer should be to the following math problem? $a + 10 = 20$, so $a = ?$ Does math have its own language?
- In what careers might you need to be a **scribe**?
- Make a list of the steps you might take to create a scaled-down **replica** of your school.

Get Ready

Fluency Warm-Up

Using Expression

To be a fluent reader, you need to read with **expression**. This is important because it makes reading more interesting and can help you better understand the selection. You can stress certain words with your voice to read with more expression.

Often, punctuation will help you read with expression. However, sometimes you'll have to decide how to read with expression on your own, based on the purpose of the sentence.

FLUENCY PRACTICE

Read each sentence with proper expression. Think about the punctuation and purpose of each sentence.

1. I can't believe you ate that entire cake by yourself!
2. When is your first day back at school?
3. Marty is going to the store to pick up some bread and milk.
4. Sharma just called to tell me that she won the race!

Get Ready

Comprehension Warm-Up

Identifying Main Idea

As you read, it is important to identify and understand the **main idea** of the selection. A topic is what a selection is all about. The main idea is the writer's most important point about the topic. The writer doesn't usually state the main idea directly. You have to figure it out by studying the details.

While you are reading, think about the details of the selection. Each sentence contains details that will help you understand the main idea.

COMPREHENSION TIP

Stop and think about the details as you read. Ask yourself questions such as these.

- Who are the characters, and what is their purpose in the story?
- What is the setting of the story, and does the setting have a purpose in the story?
- Are there ideas that are repeated throughout?
- What are most of the sentences about?
- What general point does the author want to make about the topic?

Readers' Theater

Presents
The Writing Is on the Wall
by
Justine Dunn

Cast
(in order of appearance)

Miss Williams _____

Jeremy _____

Selena _____

Colette _____

Andre _____

Museum Guide _____

Miss Williams: Please stay with your group while we are at the museum. If you are separated from your group, find someone who works at the museum.

Jeremy: How cool is this? We are going to see so many awesome things on this field trip! I hope we get to see some artwork.

Selena: I hope we get to see some rocks and gems.

Colette: I hope we get to see how the Native Americans lived. I would love to see some examples of clothing, tools, and **replicas** of homes.

Andre: I hope we get to see some bones. I love dinosaurs!

Miss Williams: You might see all of those things and more if you go back to the museum with your families. Today, we are going to the museum to learn more about ancient civilizations.

Selena: We talked about that in social studies. It sounds very interesting.

Jeremy: I can't wait to see some of the exhibits on Egypt. I wonder if we will see any treasures.

Colette: The ancient people of Egypt had many treasures. They were often buried with them when they died.

ANDRE: Does this mean we won't see any bones? Maybe I should have stayed home sick today.

MISS WILLIAMS: Actually, Andre, you should see plenty of bones. In the past, many people used bones as tools for carving and eating. Listen to the guide to find out more.

MUSEUM GUIDE: Good morning, everyone. Welcome to the Museum of Archaeology. I will be your guide today, so please feel free to ask questions along the way. I understand you are here to learn more about ancient civilizations.

(The group nods their heads.)

MUSEUM GUIDE: Well, you've come to the right place. As we like to say here at the museum, "The writing is on the wall." *(Laughs to himself.)*

ANDRE: *(whispering to Jeremy)* What did he mean by that? Do people really write on the walls here?

JEREMY: Beats me. I guess we'll have to find out. That would be so cool if we could write on the walls!

✱ SELENA: I don't think people write on the walls, you guys. He must be talking about something else.

COLETTE: I think I know what he means. I read a book about **hieroglyphics**. I wonder if we are going to see some examples of this ancient form of picture writing.

> **✱ FLUENCY TIP**
>
> Stressing words when you read will help you read with expression. For example, *I don't THINK people WRITE on the WALLS.*

Museum Guide: Did I hear someone say hieroglyphics? Do we have an **archaeologist** in the group? *(Laughs at his own joke.)*

Miss Williams: Actually, we talked a little bit about it in class. I thought it would be great for the students to see some hieroglyphs in person.

Museum Guide: Perhaps your students will be able to **decipher** some of the writings. There are many different forms of hieroglyphs that were written by many different peoples.

(The students look around at the huge stone statues that line the entrance gallery of the museum.)

Andre: Look over there at those huge stones! Why are faces carved in them?

Colette: People used to carve pictures in stone to tell stories and to record historical events. They created their own alphabets and combined symbols to form words.

Museum Guide: Sounds like you have a real interest in hieroglyphics. Maybe someday you will want to become an **epigrapher**.

Jeremy: An epigra-what? Is that someone who helps take care of pigs?

Miss Williams: No, Jeremy. An epigrapher is someone who figures out the meanings of ancient writing.

ANDRE: I want to study the bones of dinosaurs. I forget what that's called.

COLETTE: You want to be a **paleontologist**? That's great, Andre. I can't decide between that and becoming an archaeologist. Now I guess I have three choices. Becoming an epigrapher sounds interesting, too.

SELENA: I'm not sure what I want to be. I really like rocks and gems.

MISS WILLIAMS: Maybe you'd like to become a **geologist**, Selena. That seems interesting as well.

MUSEUM GUIDE: What brilliant students you have in your class!

ANDRE: Can you tell us more about those huge stones? How did you even get them in here?

COLETTE: Those look like the stones that are on Easter Island. Did you bring them here all the way from the South Pacific?

JEREMY: What's Easter Island? Do they have a lot of eggs there? How about bunnies? *(Laughs at his own joke.)*

MUSEUM GUIDE: Easter Island is famous for its enormous statues carved hundreds of years ago. Each has a long face and long body. The stones that you see here are replicas of those on Easter Island.

COLETTE: I've read a lot of books about ancient civilizations. I'm fascinated with the people and their ways of life. Selena, did you know that the ancient Maya sometimes used chocolate as money?

Selena: Now you're talking my language. I'd love to be paid in chocolate!

Jeremy: I am much more interested in trying to decipher some carvings. Can we go there next?

✻ **Museum Guide:** Absolutely. *"Write" this way! (Laughs again at his own joke as the students roll their eyes.)* Our fabulous exhibit of ancient writing includes examples from the Egyptians from Africa, the Hittites from Asia, and the Maya and Aztec from North America. But first, I'd like to show you some of the artifacts we have, including some sculptures, tools, and bones from ancient civilizations.

Andre: Did you say bones? Now you're talking! Show me the way!

Jeremy: I heard sculptures. Finally, some artwork that I can appreciate! Maybe I'll get some ideas for my own creations.

Selena: Did they include any gems in their carvings? I would love to see those.

Miss Williams: They didn't usually include gems in the carvings because they were very valuable and people would destroy the carvings to get the gems.

Colette: The carvings were used for inscriptions, recording historical events, telling stories, and labeling things with names.

✻ **FLUENCY TIP**

Sometimes when a word is written in italics, it means that you should stress that word with your voice. Read the guide's sentence, "'*Write*' this way!" The word *write* should be stressed.

Jeremy: I can't imagine carving all of those things in stone. That must have been difficult and very time-consuming. Why didn't they just write it down on paper or send an e-mail?

Andre: *(laughing)* Yeah, why didn't they just send a fax or an express package?

Selena: You two are impossible. You know very well they didn't have those things in ancient times.

Colette: A **scribe** was a highly trained person who understood the language and the scripts. At first, scribes carved on stones. Stones were hard to write on, store, and transport, so Egyptians invented papyrus for the scribes to write on.

Miss Williams: Papyrus was made from a reed plant and was similar to paper. Scribes wrote on papyrus with brushes made of reeds. The tips of the reeds were softened and shaped into a point.

Andre: Did they use lead or ink to write?

Museum Guide: Neither lead nor ink was invented yet. Scribes mixed dirt and water to use as ink. Can you imagine what it was like when it rained? Nothing like having all of your work erased in seconds.

Selena: Oh, that would be so terrible! I can't imagine living during those times.

Colette: We are very reliant on our convenient way of life, aren't we? It's hard to imagine a time without telephones, televisions, computers, and cars.

Miss Williams: When I was a little girl, we had only one television, and it didn't have a remote.

(The students gasp.)

Museum Guide: I'm a little bit older than your teacher, and I can tell you that when I was younger, we didn't even have a television. We usually listened to shows on the radio.

(The students gasp again.)

Museum Guide: OK, enough gasping for now. Save those for the astounding hieroglyphics exhibit.

(The students wander among the exhibit's ancient carvings.)

Andre: Wow, those carvings are really cool. But they are just a bunch of pictures. How can anyone tell what the carvings mean?

Miss Williams: That's where epigraphers come in. They have studied many different kinds of hieroglyphics and have learned to decipher them.

Colette: I've heard of two people that are famous for their understanding of hieroglyphics: David Stuart and Jean-Francois Champollion (zhawn-frans WAH shawm poh lee OWN). Can you tell us more about them?

Miss Williams: David Stuart lived with his parents in Mexico when he was young. David made drawings of some of the carved monuments he saw.

Museum Guide: David turned out to be a natural at understanding the hieroglyphs, or glyphs. When he was only 15, he worked as an epigrapher for a national magazine. In 1984, when he was 18, he became the youngest person to be awarded a MacArthur Fellowship.

Andre: He was only 15 when he started? That's only three years older than we are!

Jeremy: When I'm 15, I hope to be learning how to drive. I can't believe he was already figuring out the meanings of glyphs.

Andre: What about the other man, the Frenchman?

Museum Guide: Jean-Francois Champollion. In 1822, he became famous for deciphering the Egyptian hieroglyphs carved on a rock found near Rosetta in Egypt. He was only 32 at the time.

Selena: Does that help us today?

Miss Williams: Yes, it helps us very much today. Dictionaries are now available to help scholars read glyphs with ease. We would not know as much about ancient civilization without that ability.

Colette: This museum would not have as many artifacts and exhibits as it does, either. I'm really thankful for his work!

> **FLUENCY TIP**
>
> Remember to look ahead for end punctuation and change your voice for exclamations and questions.

Museum Guide: Now that you have seen and experienced a part of ancient civilization, has your opinion changed about what life was like or what you'd like to become?

Andre: Even though all of the stuff we saw today was really cool, I'll stick with my dinosaur bones. Now I know that I want to be a paleontologist.

Selena: I enjoyed seeing the large stones from Easter Island. I'm really thinking about becoming a geologist.

Jeremy: The carvings are a form of artwork, so they were my favorite part. I am still trying to imagine how they were carved!

Colette: I'm seriously considering becoming an epigrapher, or maybe even a scribe! Do you think there is still a need for them? *(The group laughs.)*

Miss Williams: Thank you so much for your help today. Now we know what you meant when you said, "The writing is on the wall."

Name _____ Date _____

Comprehension

Write your answer to each question on the lines below.

1. What is one reason ancient people carved pictures into stone?
   _____
   _____

2. Why do you think the museum has replicas of the stones found on Easter Island instead of the actual stones?
   _____
   _____
   _____

3. What did the guide mean when he said, "The writing is on the wall"?
   _____
   _____

4. Which professions were discussed in the play?
   _____
   _____

5. Why do you think Colette was so interested in ancient civilizations?
   _____
   _____

6. Why is it easier to decipher hieroglyphics today than it was during the 1800s?
   _____
   _____

7. Would you rather work as an epigrapher or an archaeologist? Why?
   _____
   _____

8. List two questions you asked yourself as you read this play.
   _____
   _____

Name _____ Date _____

Vocabulary

Write each vocabulary word on the line where it belongs.

> epigrapher   paleontologist   decipher   scribe
> replica   archaeologist   geologist hieroglyphics

1. His writing was so sloppy that it was almost impossible to _____!

2. The author of this book about volcanoes is a(n) _____.

3. My brother is building a(n) _____ of an Egyptian pyramid.

4. A(n) _____ discovered a rare fossil.

5. The walls of the tomb are covered with _____.

Extension

1. Discuss this question in a small group: "What are some ways in which monuments can be preserved?"
   - Would this be a difficult task?
   - What can you do to help?
   - How could this benefit future generations?

2. How were the glyphs of the Egyptians, the Maya, the Aztec, and the Hittites similar? How did the glyphs differ?
   - Research hieroglyphs of the Egyptians, the Maya, the Aztec, and the Hittites.
   - Find samples of the different types of glyphs.
   - Make a chart that compares and contrasts the different types of glyphs.

Sojourner Truth

Summary
"Sojourner Truth" is a six-character play about students who are working on a project about Sojourner Truth, a former slave who inspired many abolitionists.

Meet the Players

Character	Reading Level
Narrator	3.7
Kendi	3.2
Berto	4.4
Ines	4.7
Hidori	2.3
Sojourner Truth	3.6

Fluency Focus
Reading with Word Accuracy

Comprehension Focus
Summarizing

Vocabulary
antislavery
auction
autobiography
convention
involved
passion
sue

Read Aloud Tip
Introduce the fluency focus of **reading with word accuracy**. Write *reformers* and *abolitionists* on the board. Point out that good readers think about how to pronounce difficult words before they read aloud. They look at each word part and then put the parts together. Have students read each word with you, first stressing the separate syllables and then reading each whole word aloud.

Set the Stage

Teacher Read Aloud pages 110–111
This selection is about social reform in the United States and some of the individuals who fought injustice. Ask students to listen carefully as you read the selection aloud.

Get Ready

Vocabulary page 112
Use this page to introduce important vocabulary. Discuss the Word Play feature, focusing on helping students connect the words to their own background and experience.

Fluency and Comprehension Warm-Ups pages 113–114
Review these pages with students. Use the following for students who need additional help with the concepts:

- **Reading with Word Accuracy** When you come to unfamiliar words, remember to look for parts of the word that you know. Put the parts together to say a word that makes sense. Then practice saying the word. Try doing this with words from the Read Aloud, such as *petitions* and *salvation*.

- **Summarizing** Summarizing is retelling the important parts of what you read. Look at paragraph 4 of the Read Aloud. Name two or three of the most important ideas in the paragraph. Put those ideas together in a one-sentence summary of the paragraph.

Sojourner Truth *pages 115–124*

Independent Practice
Set up the groups and assign each student a part. Then have students read through their assigned parts once before small group practice begins.

Small Group Practice
Assemble the groups. You may want to use the following rehearsal schedule. Each rehearsal, which should involve a complete oral read-through, has an activity to guide students.

1. First Rehearsal: Invite students to scan the entire play to find italicized stage directions. Remind students that these directions tell actors how to speak or what to do. Discuss the reason for having the narrator and Sojourner sit separately from the other actors. Then ask students to read together as a group for the first time.

2. Vocabulary Rehearsal: Have students locate the vocabulary words used in the play and write each word on a separate index card. Then have students take turns choosing a card, reading the word aloud, and using the word in a sentence.

3. Fluency Rehearsal: Reading with Word Accuracy Before this rehearsal, review the fluency instruction on page 113. Remind students to pay attention to the Fluency Tips as they read. Then, after the rehearsal, ask each student to choose one tip and apply it to an example from the play. For example, the tip on page 117 could be used with the names *Ulster* and *Isabella* on that page.

4. Comprehension Rehearsal: Summarizing After this rehearsal, have students work together in groups to complete a Story Map that identifies important events in Sojourner Truth's life. Remind students that the Story Map should include just facts. It should not include details. Then challenge groups to use the Story Map as a guide for writing a four- or five-sentence biographical sketch of Sojourner.

5. Final Rehearsal: Observe this rehearsal, focusing on students' ability to read with word accuracy. For example, do actors look for word parts they recognize to accurately read names, such as *Van Wagener* and *Dumont*?

Performance
This is your opportunity to sit back, relax, and enjoy the performance. Encourage students to have fun while performing!

Curtain Call *pages 125–126*
Assign these questions and activities for students to complete either independently or in a group.

Vocabulary Tip
For more vocabulary practice, have students discuss the following:

- If you sit on the sidelines at a sports event, how can you still be **involved** in the game?
- What are some reasons people **sue** individuals or companies?
- Name another word that includes the prefix *anti-*, as in **antislavery**. What does the word mean?

Sojourner Truth

Set the Stage
Teacher Read Aloud

Social reformers are people who work to change things in society that they see are wrong. They are often common people who sometimes become famous for their efforts. Many of the social reformers of the past were everyday people who worked to improve the lives of others.

Throughout American history, reformers have tried to solve many problems. For many years, they struggled against the horrible injustice of slavery. As early as the 1600s, some American colonies had permitted slavery. Black slaves were brought from Africa and sold to plantation owners and other people. After American colonists gained their independence from Britain, some states, especially those in the South, continued to allow slavery.

Social reformers who worked to end slavery were called abolitionists. Both black people and white people were abolitionists. They often worked together, speaking out against slavery and sending petitions with thousands of signatures to Congress. They held meetings and conventions. Most tried to bring an end to slavery through peaceful means. They brought attention to slavery through songs, poems, and stories of how slaves were treated.

In 1833, abolitionist leaders from ten states met in Philadelphia. They created a national organization called the American Anti-Slavery Society. Their goal was to bring freedom to all slaves.

In 1844, a sea captain was attempting to help slaves escape to freedom. He was caught, jailed, and branded with the letters S.S. for "slave stealer." The poet John Greenleaf Whittier wrote a poem about the sea captain. In it he changed the brand to a badge of honor and said it stood for "Salvation to the Slave!"

Reformers continued to work for the next twenty years. The conflict over slavery led to the Civil War. Finally, President Abraham Lincoln freed the slaves in 1863. This act was what hundreds of abolitionists had worked for throughout their lives.

After the freeing of the slaves, social reformers still had a great deal of work to do. Some worked to help the slaves adjust to freedom. Others pushed for equal rights for women, especially for the right to vote. Still other social reformers wanted to help the growing number of poor people in cities.

In this play, you will read about a social reformer. Use the vocabulary and warm-ups on the next three pages to get ready to read.

Get Ready

Vocabulary

Read and review these words to prepare for reading the play.

antislavery, *adj.*: against slavery

auction, *n.*: a sale of things where buyers make bids

autobiography, *n.*: a person's life story told by the person

convention, *n.*: a large meeting of the members belonging to a group

involved, *adj.*: included or a part of

passion, *n.*: unending enthusiasm

sue, *v.*: to take a person to court for something he or she did

WORD PLAY

For more vocabulary practice, discuss the following with a partner or in a group.

- Would you rather attend an **auction** or a **convention**?
- What cause would you want to be **involved** in that you could develop a **passion** for?
- Who would write your **autobiography**?

Get Ready

Fluency Warm-Up

Reading with Word Accuracy

To read fluently, you need to know the words. Fluent readers read all the words with **accuracy**. They learn how to pronounce the words, and they learn what the words mean.

Remember to learn how to pronounce difficult words, names of people, and names of places. Do not skip words. Practice so you can read smoothly.

FLUENCY PRACTICE

Practice reading these sentences. Make sure you know how to pronounce each word.

1. We've researched the life of Sojourner Truth.
2. I was born a slave in Ulster County, New York.
3. The Van Wageners were Quakers who helped slaves.

Get Ready

Comprehension Warm-Up

Summarizing

When readers **summarize**, they retell the main points of what they have read. They take a large piece of text and condense it into just the essential facts. They don't include lots of details in a summary. They include only the critical details for supporting main ideas. They think about what the author wants them to remember.

After you read, practice retelling just the main ideas. When you can retell the story in just a few sentences, you are summarizing.

COMPREHENSION TIP

- What are the main ideas?
- What does the author want me to remember?
- Can I retell the story in just a few sentences?
- Have I answered the questions *Who*, *What*, *When*, *Where*, *Why*, and *How*?

Readers' Theater

Presents
Sojourner Truth
by
Carol M. Elliott

Cast
(in order of appearance)

Narrator   _____

Kendi   _____

Berto   _____

Ines   _____

Hidori   _____

Sojourner Truth   _____

The narrator and Sojourner should sit separately from the four friends.

NARRATOR: Our play takes place in Battle Creek, Michigan. Four friends are meeting to work on a school project.

KENDI: Our goal for this meeting is to decide how to present our project. We've each researched part of the life of Sojourner Truth. Now we have to figure out how to put the information together.

BERTO: I think we should paint a mural of her life.

INES: I think we should write a rap and perform it.

KENDI: Those are both good ideas. What do you think, Hidori?

HIDORI: I'd rather not speak in front of the class. I get so nervous. And I'm not very good at painting.

INES: Why don't we share what we've learned first? Maybe an idea will come to us as we talk about Sojourner.

KENDI: Good. I'll start since I researched her childhood. I knew that Sojourner had been a slave. But I thought only people in the South kept slaves. So I was surprised to find out that she was born in New York.

HIDORI: I thought slaves were only in the South, too. But I found out New York allowed slavery until 1827.

BERTO: When was Sojourner born?

Kendi: She never knew her birth date, but she was probably born in 1797.

Ines: She didn't know her birthday?

Kendi: No, according to my research she said—

Sojourner: I was born a slave in Ulster County, New York. I don't know if it was summer or winter, fall or spring. I don't know even what day of the week it was. They don't care when a slave is born or when he dies—just how much work he can do.

Kendi: Sojourner's mom and dad had 13 children who were all sold off to different masters. It was one of the many cruel ways slaves were treated.

Hidori: We really shouldn't be calling her Sojourner yet.

Kendi: That's right. Her name change came later. She was named Isabella, but she was called Belle most of the time. Generally, slaves didn't have last names. They used their master's last name since he owned them. In my research, I found that different sources gave her different last names.

Ines: Did slave children ever play?

Kendi: Not much. They were expected to work as soon as they could. Belle was somewhere between 9 and 11 years old when her first master died. She was sold at an **auction**.

Berto: You mean people bid on her, kind of like people bid for items at an Internet auction?

FLUENCY TIP

Practice pronouncing names until you can say each one correctly.

Kendi: Yes. Can you imagine how horrible that must have been? She was sold along with some sheep.

Hidori: Was she ever hurt as a slave?

Kendi: Yes, Belle's first master had spoken Dutch, but her second master spoke English. Her second master whipped her because she didn't learn English fast enough.

Ines: That's awful!

Narrator: The friends sat quietly for a minute. They tried to imagine what Belle had been through.

Sojourner: One Sunday morning, I was told to go to the barn. On going there, I found my master with a bundle of rods. He tied my hands together and gave me the most cruel whipping. He whipped me until I was deeply cut and blood streamed from my wounds. I still have the scars.

Kendi: She was sold two more times. Her final master was a man named Dumont. In 1810 he paid $300 for her and wrote in his record book that she was "about 13" yet "stands nearly 6 feet tall."

Hidori: That's where I take over. Belle worked faithfully for Dumont for 16 years. She worked in the house. She worked in the fields. She milked the cows. Her parents had taught her to be faithful and honest. In her mind, that meant to work hard. She did so much work that the other slaves got mad at her.

BERTO: They thought that they would be expected to work that hard, too.

HIDORI: That's right. Belle was young, and her parents were gone. She was lonely, and she was afraid of being whipped again. An older slave named Cato talked to her and helped her.

INES: Did Belle ever go to school? My research on her as an adult said that she couldn't read or write.

HIDORI: No, she didn't go to school. When she was old enough to have children, Dumont chose a slave named Tom to be her husband. Tom had been married before, but his first wife had been sold away from him.

✻ **KENDI:** The masters treated the slaves like they were cows or sheep, not people.

HIDORI: *(nodding)* Belle and Tom were good to each other. They had five children, four girls and a boy.

BERTO: But she left Tom eventually.

HIDORI: Yes, in 1817, New York had passed a law saying the slaves in the state would be freed on July 4, 1827. Dumont offered to free Belle a year early if she worked extra hard. So she did, but when the time came he didn't free her.

KENDI: That's so unfair!

✻ **FLUENCY TIP**

In Kendi's first line on this page, she tells about something upsetting. Make sure you sound disgusted.

HIDORI: So Belle decided to leave. Early one morning she simply walked away with her baby. She went to a Quaker family, the Van Wageners, who were known to help slaves.

NARRATOR: The Van Wageners listened to Belle's story. They told her that they never turned away someone in need. They offered to give her a job.

SOJOURNER: It wasn't long before Dumont found me. I refused to go back with him. To end the conflict, the Van Wageners paid him $25 for me and the baby. They told me that I was no longer a slave. I was free. But I stayed and worked as a servant for the Van Wageners to pay them back.

BERTO: Now it's my turn. Sometime before the Freedom Day, Dumont sold Belle's only son, Peter, to a man named Gedney. Gedney then sold Peter to an Alabama plantation owner who had married Gedney's sister. In New York, it was illegal to sell slaves out of state. When Belle found out that her son had been sold to someone in a southern state, she was determined to get him back.

KENDI: What did she do?

BERTO: Some Quaker families helped her hire a lawyer. She **sued** Gedney to get her son back. There were several delays. Then Gedney went to Alabama and brought Peter back to New York. There was another delay. Finally, Gedney brought Peter to court, but Peter cried out, "She's not my mother."

HIDORI: Oh, no! Belle must have felt awful.

BERTO: Luckily, the judge wasn't fooled. He could see that Peter was terrified of Gedney.

SOJOURNER: I sat in a corner scarcely daring to breathe. When the lawyers stopped arguing, I felt helpless and despised. Then I heard the judge declare that the boy be delivered into the hands of his mother. I was so thankful. Afterward, I discovered he'd been whipped several times. He was only six years old!

BERTO: Today it is common for people to sue each other, but not then. Belle was one of the first black women to sue a slaveholder and win! It shows how brave and determined she was.

HIDORI: When did she change her name to Sojourner?

BERTO: Not until 1843.

NARRATOR: After she was freed, Belle spent about 15 years working as a servant. She worked for different families. Her children grew up and got married. She was 46 when she decided God wanted her to do more with her life. She changed her name to Sojourner, meaning "one who travels." And she gave herself a last name, Truth. She would seek Truth as she traveled.

INES: When did she start speaking out against slavery?

BERTO: It wasn't long after she changed her name. She started attending large religious meetings. Most of the people were white. She would tell them about her life and the evils of slavery.

> **FLUENCY TIP**
>
> When you have several lines together, practice reading the words correctly. Then make sure you pause in the right places.

Kendi: Did they listen?

Berto: Yes, she spoke with **passion** about the cruel ways slaves were treated. Soon word spread about what a powerful speaker she was, and people wanted her to come to their meetings and speak. Many people, black and white, were working at that time to end slavery in the United States.

Ines: That's where my part picks up. As Sojourner traveled, she met famous people working to end slavery. Some of them encouraged her to write her **autobiography**.

Sojourner: A man named Olive Gilbert wrote my words down while I told my story. The book, *Narrative of Sojourner Truth: A Northern Slave*, was published in 1850.

Ines: It was a strong addition to the growing collection of **antislavery** literature. Soon Sojourner was **involved** in the movement to end slavery.

Hidori: It must have been very hard for her. Just think, she lived at a time when most famous people were white men. She was black and a woman.

Ines: That's exactly right! Back in the 1850s, women had few rights, and they could not vote. Some white women began a movement for equal rights. Sojourner decided that establishing women's rights was a cause worth fighting for, too. One of Sojourner's most famous speeches was made at a women's rights **convention** in Akron, Ohio.

NARRATOR: Hundreds of men and women were there at the convention. But Sojourner was the only black person there. Most of the men were speaking against women's rights. They argued that women were weak. They said a woman's place was at home taking care of her children. They weren't thinking about women who had been slaves—at least not until Sojourner was called to speak.

SOJOURNER: Well, children, where there is so much racket, there must be something wrong. That man over there says women need to be helped over mud puddles and such. Nobody ever helps me, and ain't I a woman? Look at me! I have plowed, and I have planted, and I have gathered. And ain't I a woman?

NARRATOR: Sojourner went on to argue each of the points the men had made. Her speech was written down and printed. More people would read it later and see how wise it was.

KENDI: When did Sojourner move here to Battle Creek?

INES: In 1857, when she was 60 years old. Two of her daughters also moved here. Her grandson Sammy loved his grandmother. For a while, she retired. She told stories, and Sammy read to her.

BERTO: But she didn't stay retired, did she?

> **FLUENCY TIP**
>
> You may want to skip unfamiliar words, but don't do it! If you don't know what a word means or how to pronounce it, look it up or ask a friend.

Ines: No, there was still too much to be done for slaves and for women. She wasn't always well accepted. Once a man criticized her, telling her that talk about slavery didn't do any good. He sneered, "Why, I don't care any more for your talk than I do for the bite of a flea." Sojourner laughed and said she hoped to keep him scratching.

Narrator: Sammy traveled with his grandmother sometimes. He read the newspapers to her. She liked what she heard about Abraham Lincoln.

Sojourner: I was glad when Abraham Lincoln was elected president in 1860. I met President Lincoln in 1864. I told him, "I never heard of you before you were talked of for president." He smiled and told me he had heard of me "years and years" before he even thought about being president.

Ines: That shows how well known she was. Sojourner really believed in a better life for blacks and for women.

Kendi: It seems to me we should speak out about such a forceful speaker.

Hidori: I agree. If Sojourner could face the kinds of crowds she spoke to, I can get up in front of our class.

Narrator: The friends agreed. They would make their project a fitting honor to the woman who had worked to help so many.

Name _____ Date _____

Comprehension

Write your answer to each question on the lines below.

1. What were two ways Belle's masters were cruel to her?
   _____
   _____

2. How did Sojourner help the antislavery movement?
   _____
   _____

3. Why do you think Sojourner went to see President Lincoln?
   _____
   _____

4. How do you think the men at the women's rights convention felt when Sojourner got up to speak?
   _____
   _____

5. Do you think Sojourner chose the right name when she changed her name?
   _____
   _____

6. What do you admire most about Sojourner Truth?
   _____
   _____

7. What are two ways in which your life would be different if you couldn't read and write? _____
   _____

8. Why do you think Sojourner was able to influence people to join the fight against slavery? _____
   _____

Name _____ Date _____

Vocabulary

Write the vocabulary word that answers each question.

> passion   convention   auction   sue
> involved   antislavery   autobiography

1. Which word names a way to sell something? _____

2. In what movement would an abolitionist participate? _____

3. What would you call an account you write about your own life? _____

4. Which word describes an intense feeling? _____

5. Which word describes a large meeting? _____

Extension

1. With a partner, choose a social reformer to research. Then present your findings to the class.

   - Find out what the reformer did and summarize it for the class.
   - Why was he or she successful at what he or she did?
   - How can you connect what he or she did to your life?

2. Discuss this question in a small group: "How would social reformers work to improve the lives of people today?"

   - Think about problems you know of in the world.
   - What could people do to help?
   - What could you do to help?

Answer Key

Survivors
Comprehension, page 30
(Suggested responses)
1. Furniture could be leaning and could fall on him.
2. They take care of Sophia, turn off the electricity and the gas, gather the essentials from the earthquake survival kit, and find food and water.
3. To minimize damage from an aftershock, they get rid of glass fragments and make sure nothing big will fall.
4. She took a first-aid class and put together an earthquake survival kit.
5. Responses will vary.
6. Responses will vary.
7. They learn that it is important to know what to do in the case of a disaster.
8. They will bolt heavy furniture to the walls.

Vocabulary, page 31
1. essentials
2. foresight
3. fragments
4. durable
5. flustered

Adaptations in Africa
Comprehension, page 49
(Suggested responses)
1. The zoo was located in San Diego, California.
2. You can get closer to animals that you would not be able to approach in the wild.
3. The animals in the zoo and in the wild did many of the same things. The giraffes used their long upper lip and their tongue to gather food. The elephants used branches to scratch themselves and used dirt to cool themselves and shoo away bugs. Animals in the zoo had someone to feed them and take care of them all the time, while animals in the wild had to care for themselves. Camels in the wild did not wear muzzles, while camels in the zoo wore muzzles.
4. Elephants can walk or run without making much noise so that their predators cannot hear them.
5. Female African elephants have tusks, but female Asian elephants do not.
6. Responses will vary.
7. Responses will vary.
8. Responses will vary.

Vocabulary, page 50
Answers from top to bottom should read as follows:
4, 6, 1, 5, 3, 2

Who Calls the Shots?
Comprehension, page 68
(Suggested responses)
1. Daniel is concerned that he is too short.
2. Pete Pituitary calls himself the captain of the endocrine "team."
3. The endocrine system consists of a group of glands that work with your bloodstream. They control your energy, your responses to the world, and your growth.
4. Three factors that can influence your height are hormones, heredity, and nutrition.
5. Daniel's doctor will track his growth to make sure that he is growing properly. Daniel's growth pattern is unique, and as long as he is healthy, Dr. Mendoza does not need to help him grow.
6. Daniel's hamburger will give him nutrition to help him grow. It provides several food groups: bread, meat, and vegetables.
7. Daniel learns that he is developing normally and that he just grows at a different rate than some of his friends do.
8. Responses will vary.

Vocabulary, page 69
Answers from top to bottom should read as follows:
2, 4, 7, 1, 3, 5, 6

The Mummy's Curse
Comprehension, page 87
(Suggested responses)
1. Jenna doesn't want to go to Egypt or go into a tomb, but her brothers are excited about it.
2. Egyptian tombs contained secret passageways and trapdoors to help protect the treasures from robbers.
3. Jenna hopes to find a ruby in the tomb.
4. The author has Anwar tell the children the scary legends to make them more interested in exploring the tomb and to warn them to be careful.
5. The red hair clip is significant because it shows where the children fall through the trapdoor and helps them be rescued.
6. Responses will vary.
7. New discoveries in tombs are interesting to people.
8. The author wants readers to wonder whether the tomb really is cursed.

Vocabulary, page 88
1. archaeologist
2. vile
3. mummy
4. tomb
5. balcony

The Writing Is on the Wall
Comprehension, page 106
(Suggested responses)
1. Ancient people carved pictures into stone to tell stories and to record historical events.
2. The stones are unique and should stay on Easter Island. Many museums can display replicas at the same time so more people can see what the stones are like.
3. The guide meant that people wrote hieroglyphs and carved pictures in stone.
4. The professions discussed in the play included archaeologist, epigrapher, paleontologist, and geologist.
5. Colette was so interested in ancient civilizations because she is fascinated with the people and their ways of life.
6. Discovering the Rosetta Stone helped people figure out what hieroglyphic symbols mean.
7. Responses will vary.
8. Responses will vary.

Vocabulary, page 107
1. decipher
2. geologist
3. replica
4. paleontologist or geologist
5. hieroglyphics

Sojourner Truth
Comprehension, page 125
(Suggested responses)
1. Belle's masters were cruel to her when they sold her at an auction and sent her away from her parents, when they whipped her until she was deeply cut and bleeding, when they treated her like one of the animals they owned instead of like a person, and when they sold her six-year-old son and whipped him.
2. Sojourner Truth helped the antislavery movement by speaking at meetings about the cruel ways that slaves were treated and by telling her story so that it could be published and added to the collection of antislavery literature.
3. Responses will vary.
4. Responses will vary.
5. Responses will vary.
6. Responses will vary.
7. Responses will vary.
8. Hearing about what happened to Sojourner made listeners realize that slaves were real people who were treated cruelly and unjustly.

Vocabulary, page 126
1. auction
2. antislavery
3. autobiography
4. passion
5. convention